The Oswego Fugues

The Oswego Fugues

Stephen Murabito

With Prelude and Postlude by Vince Gotera

The Oswego Fugues

Copyright © 2005
Stephen Murabito

Book and cover design by
Retha Schlabach Elmhorst

All rights reserved.
No part of this book may be used
or reproduced in any manner whatsoever without written permission
from the publisher, except in the case of brief quotations
embodied in articles and reviews.

Published by

~Star Cloud Press~

an imprint of
Cloudbank Creations, Inc.
6137 East Mescal Street
Scottsdale, Arizona 85254-5418

ISBN:
1-932842-04-7 — Paperback $ 22.95

StarCloudPress.com

Library of Congress Control Number: 2005920309

Printed in the United States of America

This poem is dedicated to the memories of my mother, Helen Zoni Murabito, and of my good friend, Fred Bishop.

My lungs were pumping as if they could not stop;
> I thought I could not go on, and I sat exhausted
> the instant I had clambered to the top.

"Up on your feet! This is no time to tire!"
> my master cried. "The man who lies asleep
> will never waken fame, and his desire

and all his life drift past him like a dream,
> and the traces of his memory fade from time
> like smoke in air, or ripples on a stream.

Now, therefore, rise. Control your breath, and call
> upon the strength of soul that wins all battles
> unless it sink in the gross body's fall.

There is a longer ladder yet to climb:
> this much is not enough. If you understand me,
> show that you mean to profit from your time."

I rose and made my breath appear more steady
> than it really was, and I replied: "Lead on
> as it pleases you to go: I am strong and ready."

Dante Alighieri
Inferno XXIV, 43-60
Translated by John Ciardi

He never reached the mountain. After the third day he gave up, exhausted, and the pilgrimage went on without him. He said he had the physical strength but that physical strength wasn't enough. He had the intellectual motivation but that wasn't enough either. He didn't think he had been arrogant but thought that he was undertaking the pilgrimage to broaden his experience, to gain understanding for himself. He was trying to use the mountain for his own purposes and the pilgrimage too. He regarded himself as the fixed entity, not the pilgrimage or the mountain, and thus wasn't ready for it. He speculated that the other pilgrims, the ones who reached the mountain, probably sensed the holiness of the mountain so intensely that each footstep was an act of devotion, an act of submission to this holiness. The holiness of the mountain infused into their own spirits enabled them to endure far more than anything he, with his greater physical strength, could take.

Robert M. Pirsig
Zen and the Art of Motorcycle Maintenance

This poem was completed under the auspices of grants from the Faculty Development Fund of the University of Pittsburgh at Greensburg.

For their positive feedback over the years, I thank many readers but most especially Richard Blevins, Judith Vollmer, Lewis Putnam Turco, and the late Al Poulin, Jr. I also hold a great debt of gratitude to the humanities faculty and the students at Waynesburg College (PA), where the initial final versions of *The Oswego Fugues* were first read and warmly received at the 1994 Spring Poetry Festival.

The Poet, to His Book

> Go, stubborn talker,
> Find you a station on the loud world's corners.
>
> Thomas Merton
> "The Poet, to His Book"

Go, you damned and blessed assembly of voices,
You pristine blue note of West Eighth memory.
Go, you sonata of river gull incantation,
You first sights, you lakeside songs, you last words.
Long enough have you seeped in and followed me
From Oswego to Saltsburg these fifteen years.
I first saw you in my father's garage.
We squinted, acknowledging. We sat and lit
Excalibur cigars that Christmas night
By the firewood. We drained the green bottles
Of beer, our early pencilings, our first
Measures, wild roots on unlined paper.
Now, go, fleshed out with faces, songs, and souls:
Oh, stand long on street corners until they let you in.

The Oswego Fugues

Contents

Prelude: Fugues and Fantasies by Vince Gotera   xi

The Oswego Fugues

Fugue One: Places Where the Train Stopped   1

Fugue Two: The Scene That Forgot the Man   13

Fugue Three: The Echoes We Come to Embrace   27

Fugue Four: The Wonderful Chaos   49

Fugue Five: Young Lovers Stand There Against Saint Stephen's   71

Fugue Six: The Greater Telling   85

Postlude: Crisis and Confluence by Vince Gotera   xxi

Notes   95

Stephen Murabito

Prelude: Fugues and Fantasies

Vince Gotera

NOTE: The left and right columns are spoken by the left and right hemispheres of my brain, respectively. The center column features Stephen Murabito's remarks to me about the essential features of The Oswego Fugues.

The Oswego Fugues is a cogent attempt by one of the strongest of younger contemporary American poets to pursue nothing less than—

    Whoa, whoa. Let me ask you a "cogent" question, my friend . . . are you (and me, since we're the same person) the right choice to write this introduction? I mean, really . . .

What can you possibly mean?

    Well, what do we know about fugues? Or classical music, for that matter? I know, I know . . . we're a musician, but what do we know about fugues? Or Oswego, for that matter?

I see your point. We play rock music. Though maybe I should say you play rock while I think about the blues tradition, and the emotional discordance of overlaying a mixolydian solo on the basically pentatonic matrix of rock music, so

The Oswego Fugues

we can certainly explicate the fugue from an academic point of—

        Yeah, yeah. Let's just listen to what Steve has to say on fugues.

    A fugue is a work for many voices existing in counterpoint to one another. Finally, the voices come to their conclusion in a moment of confluence called stretto maestrale. *A fugue, then, is a simultaneity of voices.*

What comes to mind here is T. S. Eliot. You'll remember, of course, that his working title for *The Waste Land* was "He Do the Police in Different Voices." What Eliot was trying to do was incorporate various voices in concert and in opposition to evoke the fragmentation of culture, society, civilization.

        What comes to mind for me is the Sixties. Especially seeing the band Stonedhenge onstage in some flatbed-truck concert in the Haight-Ashbury. *(No, folks, not the album by that name recorded by Alvin Lee and Ten Years After, but a band named Stonedhenge.)* Anyway, the lead guitarist performed an amazing solo where he played lead lines into an echo chamber and as the lines came out moments later, he played melodies in harmony and counterpoint on top of the first, and then as those returned, ditto . . . and on and on.

Stephen Murabito

Yes, that was bravura. Almost as glorious as Bach or Handel—

It was a tremendous performance for a single person, and what Steve attempts (and accomplishes) in *The Oswego Fugues* seems similarly "bravura," such stirring echo and counterpoint.

While counterpoint in The Oswego Fugues *is a counterpoint of voices, it is also a counterpoint of language styles and rhythms, establishing a continuum:*
- *Joey Bernardo, as speaker, often uses an iambic line with a variable number of feet;*
- *Others speak in dramatic prose or free verse;*
- *Some sections use nonfiction, letters, or memoirs; and*
- *Some sections use rhymed verse (for example, Joey's poem "Rebel in the Street Song," given in "Fugue #3").*

A masterful maneuver on Professor Murabito's part. Having different poetic modes for various voices is reminiscent of Shakespeare. For example, in *Hamlet,* the gravediggers speak in prose whereas the noble folk declaim in iambic pentameter.

Doesn't Eliot do something similar in *The Waste Land?*

Indeed. In that poem, the dramatic monologue that begins "When Lil's husband got demobbed," spoken by a Cockney woman in a pub, is an

The Oswego Fugues

accurately (re)constructed rendition of common lingo as practiced by the masses, whereas the (mis)adventure of the typist and the clerk, spoken by no less a figure than Tiresias, is told in a more elevated language. Pound understood these tonalities and directed Eliot, in his comments on earlier manuscripts, to excise some seedier lines in the Tiresias narration.

    And of course, Pound himself sampled a variety of voices in *Hugh Selwyn Mauberley* . . . no surprise, I suppose, that Pound's collected shorter poems was titled *Personae*.

To present these simultaneous voices, The Oswego Fugues *is structured predominantly in three columns:*
- *At the far left, column one is always the main speaker, a poet named Joey Bernardo. He has returned home to Oswego, New York, on a social mission—finally to face and express a vision he had as a child. To do this, he must find Mrs. Zicci, the old woman who held him in Saint Joseph's Church all those years ago when he had this vision. She was a visionary woman, and the elders trusted her to attend to the possessed child.*

    That makes very good sense. Today, because of Western medicine and psychology, we think of visions as abnormal. I mean, what's the first thing any psychiatrist worth her salt

Stephen Murabito

                                            will ask you if you're in therapy? "Are you hearing voices? Seeing visions?" Joey, as a child, and Mrs. Zicci, as an old woman, are connected to a primal place, where people think of visions as doors to wisdom.

Couldn't have articulated it better myself. Thus the grown-up Joey must negotiate his youthful vision with his adult perspective to—

                                            Ahem. Let the man finish, okay?

- *At the center, column two is always either a variation of Joey's voice, or dialogue between Joey and another character, or the voice of a character, or even, from outside the poem, a quotation from a poet. In a way, this is the "guest column" of the poem—monologues or "extended solos" happen here.*

                                            Cool. In the poem, for example, Joey's friend from his younger days at Oswego State University, a guy named Rossi, is dying in some hospital and sends Joey a tape recording. What Rossi says on the tape appears in the middle column—

Excuse me, as you said so succinctly, "let's let the man finish"?

- *At the far right, column three is always a chorus: These voices comment on the action, summarize, sympathize, and even at times crack jokes about what is going on. For*

The Oswego Fugues

example, as the poet recalls working through an early period of selfishness as a poet (contrary to his desire now to have a "social mission" and "speak for" others in Oswego), the chorus more or less berates him.

Whew. That's like Faulkner's "A Rose for Emily," in which the narrator is some kind of collective voice for the town, giving us a sense of the citizens' widespread outrage against the old lady's actions, although they nevertheless respect her precisely because she *is* a lady, because of her breeding.

This third column goes beyond Faulkner's device in that story. These voices are privy not only to Joey's actions but also to his inner thoughts and desires, his falterings and inconsistencies.

So column three is something like the narrators of Larry Heinemann's novel *Paco's Story* . . . the ghosts of Paco's decimated unit. Paco is the only American soldier left alive in his unit after a firefight in Vietnam, and the ghosts of his comrades follow him, narrating and commenting on what he does, what he thinks, what he loves, what he hates. As a matter of fact, I'm sensing connections with other recent narratives, especially ones in verse. Two that come to mind are Vikram Seth's *Golden Gate,* a novel told in several hundred

Stephen Murabito

Yes, Professor Murabito's use of the word "chorus" above is revealing. His third-column characters essentially form a Greek chorus. In the early Greek tradition, before Aeschylus, four festivals a year in honor of Dionysus were performed in Athens by a chorus, often made up of prominent Athenians. Legend tells us that a member of the chorus, named Thespis, separated himself from the chorus to sing in dialogue with it—an agon or dramatic conflict—using different masks to portray different characters.

Exactly. Aeschylus was the first Greek dramatist to capitalize on Thespis's innovation, incorporating two actors and thereby allowing the possibility of an antagonist—who would sing the "anti-agon"—poised against the hero, or protagonist. And later dramatists, such as Sophocles, expanded the ranks of the actors.

Yes and no. Column one is always Joey as protagonist; column two is sometimes Joey acting as his own

sonnets, and *Time's Fool* by Glyn Maxwell. Neither of those, however, use Steve's notion of a "chorus" in his third column.

Ah, and so we have the word *thespian* for actor. Very cool.

So what is Steve's contribution in *The Oswego Fugues*? If column three is the chorus, then are column one and two the protagonist and the antagonist?

The Oswego Fugues

antagonist. At other times, we hear less central characters—Joey's Uncle Stosh, Mrs. Zicci—in column two. Sometimes the chorus in column three plays antagonist to Joey, deflating his complacency—

Hold on a minute. Aren't we getting ahead of ourselves? The good people "out there" haven't read *The Oswego Fugues* yet.

Absolutely right. Read on, gentle people . . .

And we'll see you on the flip side. Watch for the afterword . . .

Stephen Murabito

The Oswego Fugues

Fugue One:

Places Where the Train Stopped

The Oswego Fugues

Stephen Murabito

I

> Ramon Fernandez, tell me, if you know,
> Why, when the singing ended and we turned
> Toward the town, tell why the glassy lights,
> The lights in the fishing boats at anchor there,
> As the night descended, tilting in the air,
> Mastered the night and portioned out the sea,
> Fixing emblazoned zones and fiery poles,
> Arranging, deepening, enchanting night.
>
> Oh! Blessed rage for order, pale Ramon,
> The maker's rage to order words of the sea,
> Words of the fragrant portals, dimly-starred,
> And of ourselves and of our origins,
> In ghostlier demarcations, keener sounds.
>
> Wallace Stevens
> "The Idea of Order at Key West"[1]

I see
my Uncle Stosh

stumble from the bathroom there,

the wall, immaculate,
coming up on him quickly.

As I drive toward the home,
his eyes pure Warsaw, 1910,

I know he sees
his Vistula River
behind thick frames.
I know he does, but to say it, and—

Oh, rockface/
referentiality:

The Oswego Fugues

                        It's past the Genesee and
                        Polish vodka the uncle
                        pours in the days he
                        has the house on Rome St.
                        and sings, *Sit and drink*
                        schnapps! his stories
                        hovering in smoke. It's
                        past Vona's, before the
                        visit, quarters in the
                        jukebox, a freshly lit
                        cigar, two lounge lovers
                        dancing Tuesday away. The
                        poet knows their names
                        as they kiss, sees her job
                        promotion in how she taps
                        the Salem. Now, at the All
                        Saints Home, he stands
                        staring at the fountain.
                        Oh, to tell anyone it is
                        the same water, through
                        time, his uncle touches
                        on a rainy apple on the one
                        tree, in the sweet Polish
                        fog of home, the city he's
                        forgotten. *That's* where it
                        is, begins, always begins
                        in the young poet's mind.

And when I visit,
he wants
a cigar.
Okay,
if I can.
But the doctor
forbids it,   Hoyo
                         Excalibur
                         (ring number fifty-two),[2]

and if I sneak in
one more bottle
of God's Luksusowa,
the nurse will say,

                         You just don't understand, sir;
                         his system just can't take it.

I show him an old map
of Poland, circa 1912,
a list of names, the families,
around the edges.

Stephen Murabito

*I wrote
them down,*
I say.

The steadied finger now
begins to trace the places where
the Warsaw train would stop.

*My girl,
Ewa Zoniski . . .*

His eyes blaze brown, as if
she lives there still—
blue line, black dot. He
shakes, but the stories
are still clear as water,
themselves sources,
springs, faces, voices
in the human fugue in the
mind of the young man.

Her father's vodka,
the two brown bottles:
She puts them into
a burlap sack,
her hand on his.
He'll leave to fight
and never make it back.

*Oh, Joey,
her eyes,
were dark,
like lights.
I kissed her
at the station.
She took the vodka home.*

The words, and worlds,
how it's always been—this sunshine—
all rivers between us.

I see him   The nurse arrives, says,
at that station   *He has to go*
but cannot   *back to his room, sir.*
say more.   *It's best like this, sir.*

The Oswego Fugues

His face changes
from the window
to reflect
now into
his insistence.

And the quick wink
of a lie, an agenda.

Oh, that's called
human sweetness.

more a human echo
      (a
        weakness,
    a
silence).
The words
are meaningless,

spiraling down
to old shoes,

a taste
gone from

the tongue—a kiss,
by an apple tree.

The round black bread
and her potato vodka—
I touch his hand
and start to see
the face he saw that day.

And now,
he's out of stories
and won't look up.

Schmoke scigar?
he pleads to me—

*Now, you know you can't smoke
those cigars outside because
you kept letting them fall all
over the ground. Besides, the ladies
are all complaining—maybe later,*
the nurse spits out, her lips hard-lined.

*Today, the trees are blooming . . .
When we go outside . . . And besides, sir,
the ladies were all just complaining . . .*

I have map, he says to her
like a man with foreign currency,
a man sure it must be, it must be . . .

In his uncle's eyes,
he can see the red tree,
smell the air. But he
fights it, fights it.

He has seen souls forever.
She is beautiful, brown
curls, eyes blacker than
the great forest.

Stephen Murabito

The ancient map
remains in his lap.
His hands are fallen bone.
Its faded pinks and blues
are the ghosts of roads
and cities. The young man
takes the map and sees
his uncle turn to board the
train: Oh, *The apparition
of these faces in the
crowd . . .*3

And I can see,
the hands that folded this
over and over again.

Stosh can't see the words,
the names of towns,
yet he tells his story
to thin air, then stops:

I know nothing.

The voice of a man
giving in, giving up.

The young man has heard
that voice echo for years.

The water, though,
we share at bedside
is good, is succulent.
He drinks through his closed eyes.
But it is not Vistula,
which may as well
move like clouds,
like Jordan past Jericho,
oh, past Succoth,
and past Beth-shean—
north to the Sea
of Galilee.

II

I see the old
black-and-white

photo of Grandma,
circa 1930,

in Oswego, New York's
Dante Alighieri Club.

After his visit, he is home
for coffee with his father.

After biscotti, it's photo
albums, the father laying
faces down like cards in a
game of solitaire.

The Oswego Fugues

I stare until
she's only eyes,

the human face
I can't forget.

Oh, not this radiance.

His entire life has been
eyes, arms, and stories.
Yet how to speak it?

He sees a chest of drawers,
dark brown mahogany,
Stickley. It's in Grandma's
garage, old books like its
faithful surrounding it.
There are two rockers
although nobody remembers
her in anything but a
kitchen chair, the Viceroy
lit, Sinatra on WSGO, the
hot day, fresh sauce on the
stove, the smell consuming.
There's a breeze. The boy
touches that rake, that old
chair. He's disappeared.
Now, boxes, tools. This,
a scattering. But this,
his endless beginning.

Oh, something remains,
yet all these things have gone
with her, with all of them.

Oh, Imogene Missina.
Oh, Santa CasaVecchio,
Nunzia Bernardo.
Oh, Angelina, Estella, Antonia—
all the sisters, friends,
their faces olive, resilient
in a banquet photo:
Their faces gone but that calling

roundness

white shirts
fresh dresses

Stephen Murabito

smoke
kitchen

veal
coffee

stories
humor

St. Joseph's
Uncle Tony

Teresa Brewer on WSYR
as smoke is curling,
laughter rising,

a Saturday night,
such human warmth,

olives in a bowl
on the table,

Canada Dry
Ginger Ale,

shining plates,
faces,

hands,

chairs—

defeat of

narration.

This fragmentation against
his mother hearing his
three voices singing in the
practice room. It is July
of 1962. Against the sudden
Oswego rain, he puts
words to the Mozart duet,
musical memory rising with
steam from her stilled
ironing board. But he won't
sing for her when she asks.
Still, there are strange
words, words she tells his
father the boy simply
shouldn't know.

And still, the young man
fights it, fights it off—

At the beautiful buffet,
the tall green bottles
are too big for his small
hands, but the maps of
Canada, and those old
red rubber stoppers
fascinate him to singing.
Adults pause, listen from
a distance, shake away
the possibility of what
they have half-heard,
and step back into the
dance of their lives.

The Oswego Fugues

III

> The tackle box with Uncle
> Stosh's White Owls sits in
> the ashes, stands the test
> of fire the night the '59
> Continental melts. Halves
> of the family meet—Polish
> and Italian, a confluence
> of astonishment as the old
> man collapses in the orange
> shadows, pounding his fists
> into the hot lawn.

I see him when
I am a boy,
his tortured soul   My father says,
flung up to ash: *Son, I turned you away,*
A sudden rootwork   *my hand on your sweet-smelling head,*
of agonized red   *the firmness of love*
light splits   *through such tragedy.*
the sky.   *I'm sorry. I know you saw it all.*

Years later,
I ask about the fire.
Stosh looks me in the eye
but squints beyond the pain.

> *Time, time, Joey, that's the thing:*
> *You can't let it slip all away*
> *even though you still know*
> *it is—the sonovabitchin' thing.*

I see him under his pear tree,
his head falling,
his eyes and hands closing,
his fingers folding
to knot under blossoms:

And I swear I hear him breathing.

IV

The music of these Iroquois street names—
Oneida, Onondaga, Cayuga,
Mohawk, and Seneca: Five nations hanging
on tough in this February blizzard.
Oh, the ice fishing's good, the brandy flame,
and Socrates, my massive Newfie dog,
plows along with me: Oswego, I sing
with your white wind: town, lake, snow, fish—a fugue.

Who else will seek your voices through this storm,
the whiteout's sheets of music become arms?
Who else will seek your breath by jagged rocks
and hear in it a prelude of blind trout?
I drill the hole through ice, and if I fall,
this ancient breed will howl me back to life.

V

Now, the hot minestrone
with my Aunt Yolanda.
We wait out the storm.
WSGO says it'll get worse.
Oswego is a frozen
sprawling of streets,
twisted like dead riverbeds,
and my hands go weak
in the blasting cold.
Yes, the wind sweeps
you into song.

He turns five, stares
into the strong hands
of his uncle, all
smiles and sweet cigar
smoke, hefting the kid up,
a weightless rising.

Waiting it out
in midday darkness,
I clean the three lake perch
and one brown trout I pull
from the frothy blackish-green.
Their mouths are singing,
frozen in insuck.
Their eyes are clear
as any thought I've had.
One stares through me,
and on to perpetuity.
The other stares in opaque grace
reminding me of my runny news.

The Oswego Fugues

Oh trout, a blue and red
that's deep beneath the green
and then a flash of gold
to name your shadow reappearances.

Now in the house, we eat sliced provolone
on warm bread while the fish bakes.
She'll drop the rigatoni soon.
But first, she pours
short breaths of Beam,
no ice.

She tells about the time
Stosh sat in this same chair
and claimed he couldn't see:

> *The tears fell to his bread, Joey.*
> *That's how I knew God was talking to me.*
> *It was all I could do to call 9-1-1.*

But you, my love,
the snow is blinding;
you, my love,
such a white wait for me:
The distance between us,   Oh, their love is *Like gold*
                                             to an aery thinness beat.[4]
between the souls I've loved,
is all I see.

VI

Socrates and I
move through familiar streets,
moonlit black and white,
and glistening silver-red.
He knows the smell of step on step,
how time reduces way to home,
how we will stand as we've always stood,
to be held by you and the night,
the snow of our lives on your fingers.

The ice   Oh, but he's *more like*
on the dog's legs   *a man / Flying from*
catches a star   *something that he*
and says to me   *dreads than one / Who*
that I have spent my life   *sought the thing*
somehow running from this thing. *he loved.*[5]

Fugue Two:

The Scene That Forgot the Man

The Oswego Fugues

Stephen Murabito

I

> For *place*, itself, is always a kind of motion,
> A part of it artificial and preserved,
> A part born in a blur of loss and change—
> All places in motion from where we thought they were,
> Boston before it was Irish or Italian,
> Harlem and Long Branch before we ever knew
> That they were beautiful, and when they were:
> Our nation, mellowing to another country
> Of different people living in different places.
>
> Robert Pinsky
> *An Explanation of America*[1]

Dear John:[2]

You know we got married and moved from Oswego to Pittsburgh, where I now sit at my desk writing this. I went back home last month and ever since then feel pulled like river current to return again. There's something there I know I've got to do. That's why I'm writing. I've been thinking a lot about you, my teacher, my friend.

As you could no doubt guess, the first thing I did was go back to the old neighborhood, West Eighth and Oneida. With a six-pack of Genny I bought down at Vona's Restaurant, I walked up to the corner. The old store is an apartment house now, doors half on hinges, a garbage dump outside, the lawn more brushed dirt than grass. It was—what?—*collapsed* is all I can come up with. I thought I'd be moved, want to ask the folks on the Eighth Street side (where we lived) to let me take a little tour; I was even going to give them the six-pack for the pleasure. But standing in the back yard, I felt nothing—that is, until I went around the corner and saw the one thing that hadn't changed, the number *159* in its slanted script along the side of the front porch.

The Oswego Fugues

    I saw before me a swirl of voices, stories, lives, and one in particular. But I thought my chest would explode, so I tucked the six and made it to Seventh Street, to your old place, where I opened a cold bottle on the steps. I sat there watching the icy sweat on the brown glass. Man, everything was alive, alive in vibrant reds and greens, and those houses were so tiny compared to the ones I see now around Pittsburgh. A woman, her face ancient, lined like a map, rapped at your old window (that crack's still there as if it had a mind of its own).

    I turned. She scowled. She rapped again, her fist nearly balled up, her one knuckle big like a man's. She jerked her head, motioned for me to leave. All of it was wordless, a set of glaring gestures. It was hard to believe that the same porch held such great welcome in the past. When I turned again, she'd disappeared into the framed darkness.

    After she chased me away, I got down to about West Third Street, sat on the steps of the First Presbyterian Church, and looked back toward the neighborhood, now beyond the horizon. I was missing it already. The Molinaris, the Di Mieros, the Kings, the hospital further up from your old place.

    Hey, I see the time we broke up laughing in that great kitchen of yours, every pore, every ledge, every angle bursting with a wok, a pan, a loaf of bread, some fruit, some coffee, a plate, silverware, mixes—that kitchen, that great openness, that great hospitality in process.

    I see the day you made six or seven different kinds of tea—red, yellow, green, orange, brown, maroon, and one, I swear, it was some funky shade of purple, some unknown hue of red like the sunset over Lake Ontario.

    You told April and me: "Life is so predictable, so mundane, so full of assholes: This is to complicate our lives; let's complicate our lives!" The whole thing struck me as so absurd. I saw titles like *The Many Teas of Tuesday Afternoon.* I saw it on a stage: The sophisticated man, purposely trying to complicate his life—I don't know, to flee his past or something—

is kicked out of a diner for frustrating the waitress over all of the various teas he tries to order. I must have been exhausted with work and complications of my own, but I laughed so hard, man, so damned hard.

I see us on your porch. We looked across the street, and you know I told you about growing up in that place, about the house over there, the day the young boy drowned. We heard his mother screaming up in the emergency tunnel of the hospital off Seventh. I just never mentioned that I was nowhere in earshot. Truth is, as word spread, all the rest of the kids ended up by the big mailbox on Seventh and Oneida. I fell to my knees then rose in the shade of Mrs. Molinari's side yard. I began to choke as if I were drowning.

She came out and said, "Oh, honey, what happened?"

Those two voices together—her kindness and the mother's terror—and the siren that stopped yet still howled in my ears—I swear, I knew all of the details, how he was fine, swimming with the other kids, just hanging onto a log. Then his head hit it, and he was under. I saw it, John, saw it clear as day.

She asked again. "Honey, can I call your mother?"

"I don't know, Mrs. M.," I finally told her. "I don't know what happened." And I ran by the others with their bicycle wheels stilled, their baseball gloves dangling; I ran back to West Eighth and Oneida, where I only wanted to be a kid, a normal kid.

And I see myself, all our books piled between us, telling you about the hoods, the day, right across the street again, when this big one pounded a terribly skinny one. It must've been January or February of 1964. I must've been all of eight. Back then, we called them *hoods,* and for us kids, man, that meant they were the meanest boys alive. They'd hang out with their greased hair, leather jackets, vicious faces, and those pointed black shoes. They even wore them in the snow. Just the name *hoods*—it meant something; it rushed through us.

The Oswego Fugues

After that first fight, the two of them vowed to return the next day. To me, this meant that I had to be as tough as they were, so I stole a pack of Winstons and lit one up in the back yard. Then, I went down in our basement and looked at one of my dad's old *Playboys* and thought myself strong for standing face-to-face with that waterfall of naked beauty.

They met and fought in the bitter, sunny, hard-packed, salty snow. I bit my tongue, tasted blood on choked breath; their cries were a pulsing in my heart. They danced and swore, punched and kicked, fell and somehow rose again, poets with an obscene cadence.

But I never told you that I saw it, saw it seconds before it happened: The big one slipped because those slick, ominous shoes gave on the ice. The skinny kid gave a scream of anger, anguish, and attack—I've never heard anything like it since. The bigger hood wailed under the cracking, brutal blows, his face exploding under the sudden brass knuckles. My heart pierced then that the world was a frozen place of stained red snow, a place of terror and beauty and hatred and foreseen yet somehow still utterly imperceptible quickness.

I see myself telling you about the time the big kids in the neighborhood caught a giant mud turtle and began to torture it for three days. There were constant updates: Where was the turtle? Who had it? What new torture was in line for it today? Then I snuck out one night, stole the turtle from Doug Hillman's back shed, and ran with it to the river's edge behind First Street. I tossed the whole bag in, my heart pounding like the wind.

I told you—April had heard it all before—how I stood there watching the bag swirl out until I swore the turtle came loose. I laughed when you said that you didn't want to hear any more neighborhood stories until I started writing them down. I mean, even though I couldn't tell you all I saw, you still knew that *place*, place would be the starting point.

Stephen Murabito

    John, thanks. I did write it down; I am writing it down still; I think I'll be writing it down for the rest of my life. Those initial stories are the toughest to write, all because of the ironic power and weakness of language to do what we *need* it to do for those about/for whom we write. I began to see—perhaps, strange as it sounds, in those six or seven different kinds of tea—a connection between genres, something you insisted on from the start: Narration, poem, line, word, song, release, turning point—they all share a common center. It's my only chance, John.

    It was good tea, man. The beer was cold, too. What else can a teacher do but put elements and possibilities in front of students who are willing to consider those possibilities? That plus never stop considering them him or herself? There's a spark that flies; there's a spark that keeps flying. It's made of stores and stolen cigarettes, sirens and pointed shoes; it's made of nude women emerging from the single-bulbed shadows of a stony basement; and it's made of glorious walks home over the empty streets of Oswego, New York, because you swear at last that a turtle swam free in the blackest water God ever made.

Take care,
  Joey B.

II

                        a kind of motion . . .[3]
in the mind never stopping
                    born in a blur
I reach for the soil
                  of loss and change—/
of West Eighth and Oneida
                  . . . before we ever knew/
as these hands are old enough
                    That they were beautiful . . .
that too much falls

back to the ground

The Oswego Fugues

III

I can barely recall
why I'm here

in my office today,
the very place slipping away.

And these woods, too, begin
to fade to a pulling—

all these memos, appointments
against the mind's lake wind.

I forget the committee meeting.
I forget the twins' prescriptions.

I eat my lunch,
the simple grounding things—
my wheat bread, my cold turkey,
my cheddar cheese, and a drink
of water.

Like all the places he's
been the minute his
people move in his mind.

How can you be in one
place with so many souls
pulling?

He thinks of fishing
with his Uncle Stosh, the
thick hands baiting the
hook. Oh, lures and
lakes shining still.

Oh, it'd be sweeter on
the fort cliff or at the
river's edge in Oswego.

One day, in his office,
he sees his uncle fall
and break his hip on the
cellar steps. He goes
down for a beer, chilled
in the darkness against
the stone wall. He lies
in the hospital, the pain
becoming an entity, a
place. He shouts that
there are no children,
that the rooms will kill
him: *I have no place,* he
cries, *no place.* He is
given shots that drive
him to a shoreline of
sleep, two boys fishing,
one keeping secrets.

Stephen Murabito

IV

I see a single glove,[4]
its fingers lying curled
as if still filled by flesh.

And these years later, it is mine,
my own worn glove, without my hand.
I find it on the floor and see

back to Chianti with John Logan
at a SUNY conference,   Brockport, NY: 1979.
his face a ruddy stanza.

He says that learning verse with Lew Turco
will surely do me justice
in the end, in the *long run,*

because he teaches
that form is vital,
but a language that somehow

is working against it
is still more vital when
it flows from a place

knowledge has the wisdom   Turco says,
to ignore at times.   *Don't be fooled*
That's inspiration, he says.   *by Dylan Thomas's*
                                       vast energy;
And for the first of many times,   *he's a master,*
I wonder if words have the power   *able to abandon*
to say what mind and soul need said. *himself into measure.*

                                         In the late afternoon
But you are right.   *light / even our human*
From place to place,   *feet / start halos in*
my life's a long run back—   *the sand: / soft*
                                         flashes of mind.[5]
but now, I'm asking you
my burning student question:
What's it like to *place* a word so perfectly—

The Oswego Fugues

    I mean, your *halos in the sand*
    or your *soft flashes of mind?*
    And you tell me something I forget,

    something small and incremental,
    of baby steps to miracles,
    of life with pen in hand.

    When I leave work
    and walk
    into the woods,
    I'm at this place,
    a place between all places,
    so today I call it Logan's Creek.
    Beneath
    the Loyalhanna Dam,
    where the fish
    bunch up,
    a great blue heron stands
    for hours near the rocks
    as if she is
    painted against the pines
    that line the bank,
    painted against the greying sky
    and misty bridge beyond her.
    In the water,
    I see all water,
    and the pale sun here is a salmon moon
    up in Oswego.
    The world has turned
    to fish that live
    a silver running,
    a lifetime running,
    a darting deep in sun pulse
    of twisting silhouettes
    the way
    places ghost
    and bolt through us
    when we travel through them.

    Oh, Oswego in the Pennsylvanian woods:
    First Street along the Kiski River,
    River Street on a Friday night,
    the Ferris Wheel spilling dancers
    along the muddy Loyalhanna: We
    stagger our ways to the lake.

    He is a man
    along a riverbank
    starting a fire,
    but the fire burns
    inside a circle of
    shoreline stone.

Stephen Murabito

These are our knotted fires,
our twisted, orange shoreline lights,
our philosophies rolled and rolled
long past reason to a paper-thin glow,
then grey ashes dancing,
rising like fireflies,
our questions beyond midnight.
West, Claude, Egger, Reb, Chip—
beer by the rocks,
Labatt's like breath,
no wind from Ontario,
a patient blackness like the night itself,
a few of us in, under, out,
dried and back to the fire again.
Someone descends the cliff,
laughing down the rocks,
cold fish sandwiches,
ketchup spread hysterically
with a *Seagram's 7 Crown*
key ring tab.

These are our fallen fires,
flat, rooty at sunrise,
my white jacket blackened with ash,
the silent ride home,
the sudden glare at Mitchell Street
of the utter blueness of Ontario,
and someone tells about Susan Todd,
how she swims out beyond us
as we tread gently on the deep fear under our feet,
how she calls to us but keeps on going,
out to the foggy horizon
of our squinted amazement,
a power, strength,
beauty and grace
returning to stand there,
breathing steady,
laughing and singing,   He strides to his car
striding out of her knee-deep water.   to get a warm coat.
                                        The PA rain is cold.

   I turn
   to see

   the pole
   the line

   the still
   water, my

The Oswego Fugues

tackle box:
Oh, the scene

that forgot
the man

who forgot
the music—

not like the boy
who chooses to push

it all away.

Oh, touch of pole,
and then the cast

like every one
before it under this

sudden sun
I'll always name Oswego.

This against his First Grade teacher hearing him play the class piano. She stands over his shoulder, and he won't go on, the fingers freezing across tongue upon tongue of what's possible against the fading echo of the harp in the deep wood of the fall of 1962.

V

Oh, we are all here,
in the old church—
St. Joseph's.

We fold our hands
on silent knees,
and I don't understand.

I see the choir stand
although I'm nowhere near them.
They offer up their solemn dirge.

And I hear the Latin words begin,
but then a flash to the coffin,
and time has closed around

their words that fly up with smoke
as the men are bunched outside—
yet everyone is still inside the church.

The one place,
the one time he
can't push away.

He is only six.

Stephen Murabito

I see her life turn to smoky roses,
the men who sing her food and sewing,
the simple things that made her time.

Yet an altar boy still bears the cross,
and now the dead ascend the steps,
and move unseen through the center aisle.

We are the light surrounding them.
and I don't know what to do
with such a white-hot pull.

They climb
the church walls.

*Look, look, know: Know
this: This is your
light, blinding white
and black.*

And for a flash,
there is a heaven,
but it is here

in Oswego, New York.

Faces disappear
in a small church,
where he falls weeping.

And the visionary Mrs.
Zicci understands his
crying voice as she is
let through to hold him.

*It'sa ok. Ita leave you now.
Ita come back somma day.
Shh . . . somma day, you know,
anda you tella everybody.*

And we are left
here to live
with and without the dead.

Oh, full of grace,
full of grace,
full of human grace.

The Oswego Fugues

VI

Olives in a giant crock,
the sweet black diamonds.
As I eat one, I see
the old Sicilian woman,
her hands shaking as she fills
a bucket. I run away.

In the weeks following,
it all seems forgotten
until he stands on the
sawdust behind the meat
counter, where his
father waits on people.

Saby, a pound of my provolone!
Mr. Zicci calls out
as I round the corner
and fly out the door.

But I stop in Oneida Street
and turn to watch my father:
He lays the full moon of cheese
on the old Toledo scale.

For his customer,
his smiling customer.
And others wait behind.

But there is no more
pastrami to slice, Dad,
no more sausage to make,
or bacala to weigh
on white paper
at Christmas time,
no more fresh sausage to curl onto the scale,
no more sawdust to spread at closing time,
no lines of knives to sharpen,
no Ballantyne Ale to stock in display cases,
no local bowling scores over apples
on a winter night.

Yet there,
for a flash,
a man so present
that he defines the place
on the faces of Mr. and Mrs. Zicci,
who come out born in their white packages,
who come out laughing loaves of bread,
who come out weightlessly
and never see me there

even though I will always be here

stunned then fleeing
from West Eighth and Oneida.

He'll always be
on that corner.

Fugue Three:

The Echoes We Come to Embrace

The Oswego Fugues

Stephen Murabito

I

                                          "Here! Here! Before you go!
                                          I *made* this for you!"

                                                                A child to her parent,
                                                                 Oswego, NY[1]

                                        Perhaps, sometime, out of the
                                 fragments one little by little brings
                                 to oneself, something like a world
                                 will be discovered in the overall
                                 perspective—but that is still a good
                                 way off.

                                                             Rainer Maria Rilke[2]

Here, in her warm kitchen   In Slickville, PA.
alive with a Bach fugue,
the cello soft, the violins behind it,
the snow melts off our boots
to the sudden acoustic perfection
that hits me like the other world.

The question comes   Again, it's in
                                                               his mind and blood
            Is it possible?   to find the words.

            Is it possible?
            Is it possible?

It pulses through
the *adagio,*
a perfect walk through sound to light.

            Is it possible?
            Is it possible?
            Is it possible?

The Oswego Fugues

Mrs. K. loves her son:

> *Come, Joey, sit, listen. You'll like this.*
> *It's Stanley's string quartet.*
> *Oh, do you hear that? There.*
> *I don't know why. But I love that part.*
> *I play this whenever it snows.*

> Bach is a living
> thing, a human
> turning, a
> returning, voices
> made, voices
> remade.

I see
her eyes

but have gotten
beyond language.

> The human fire:
> Water, color, life
> its own dimension.

Inextinguishable.

And to think we've come here
to pick up raffle tickets
for Saint Sylvester's festival.
But here, yes, here
is a sacred thing, an opus stretched
over the yellow kitchen table:
a thin sheet of strudel dough
draping down like a curtain.

> The opaque light
> behind it or within
> it or coming from
> it, a singularity, a
> simple goodness
> made from thickened
> hands to fill this
> place with his
> undying questions:
> What does it mean?
> Can words begin—?

She moves around
in her own fine time,
and the curtains are alive
in an echo from the walls.

Stephen Murabito

She is a voice
in the fugue of my running:

> *He left, Joey, and there was nothing*
> *I could do about it. He was*
> *for just a second so . . . absolutely*
> *with me on that couch. And then, that*
> *helplessness took him away. I told him,*
> *Shh . . . it's okay if you have to go.*

I want to ask
a thousand questions
as if each answer
just one,
will be that underpinning,
those barest bones I need.

But here it happens quickly,
and I know it's death again,
the glimpse of it
I've spent my life running away from,
from snow to Bach and strudel,
from electric light of cars that pass
in shadows gone from walls
once the boy I am returns home,
from tone of voice
imparting life story
to voice of strings,
each calling me to
this water-light underfoot
on sunken green tiles,
from the sudden traditions
which fall through human hands,
the heart comprehending,
giving in the absorption
of the hand on hand
I see on that couch.

The question returns   A motif in the soul,
in the time of the music: voices made, remade.
                                                       But words pulsing
          Is it possible?   hard seem nothing
          Is it possible?   but verges.
          Is it possible?

The Oswego Fugues

                                                                                    Yes, the light from
the dough. Yes, the
smile of the
mother's face. Yes,
yes, the sweetness
of merciful knowing
in the widow's eyes,
yes: The human
softness of the word
itself, hardly
a word but some
music born of our
memory of faces.

She's talking,
by now pure sound,
which could be
an explanation
of my life,
one bursting toward
a music of knowing.

This is what we make,
what we become,
spaces in between,
as surely as the music
is made of its own pauses,
the richest silences
it surrounds—

gatherings, yieldings,   voices made, remade:

                                                                                                   Oh, rockface/
referentiality.

At the festival,
her strudel disappears.
The Luzinski sisters
polka every dance,
never out of breath like me,
but steady smiles—
one unending face.
Oh, the dancers,
here they come again,
this time with their mother
and the two granddaughters
who don't understand exhaustion,
all of them stepping, stopping, stepping,
twirling to new points in the circle.

Stephen Murabito
II

I am twenty-two, powerful,
never a thought,

What am I saying?
To whom do I speak?

The perpetual music
of my own voice

as I bite through ice to Beam,
where my ideas can't hide.

I read my Pound, my
Stevens, and Eliot,

and my steadfast
Book of Forms,[4]

where possibility lives
while I think   the world   in fours   or fives   or sixes.

I'm a real strategist,
intuitive craftsman.

I want the purest flame,
the ultimate pour.

I catch
fragments
like smelts
in nets.

The words he learns
to make, oh, to roll
like cigarettes, to
inhale and burn
away—he loves them
for themselves.

Speech? Words?
Faugh! Who talks
of words / and
love?! [3]

Look, the syllables
fly from his fingers!

Oswego, NY: The Wheel,
down by the river
running north, a
singing blackness
still moving years
past its own history
of rapids and falls
dynamited, tamed.

The Oswego Fugues

And Friday afternoon
spins to an academic close.

Our books are on
the Wheel's black ledges,

the snowy night a hope
filled with voices we'll let fall

and catch us just because
this is the run of college,

a human fugue of sex and thought
to dreams of love, this state we make

to remake ourselves.

Ah, this bar has
fantastic windows!
You see Ontario's
whitecaps break from
black water.

*Fred, Jack, Jimmy,
Claude, Chip, Egger, man.
Hey, outside.
I rolled a few
suitable for the wind.*

Stoned, I think
myself smart,

the world never
slowing down

into anything
but lines of verse.

I never think
of why I write.

I breathe indulgent sonnets,
wail my egotistical

villanelles, but marry
failure to possibility

for the love of sound
that promises to blast

How deeply can one
November night be
sucked into their
lungs, for crying
out goddamned loud?

He's absorbed in
infrastructures,
the woven
measures themselves.

Always the pushing,
so many pencils
pushed to a flat
dullness in his
hands. But, of
course, he's really
running like a
blind trout.

Stephen Murabito

through every blackness known.
But now, the self emerges

from title through quatrain to coda.

                                                              Fucker's been out
                                                              howling in the
                                                              streets tonight,
                                                              Mum, writing on
                                                              paper bags again.

                        Rebel in the Street Song

                        By visions of clarity and some other entity,
                        The price of love is too high.
                        And what does it say to me?
                        But that's all it can ever be,
                        So just let loose with a sigh.

                        Raise your voices, and scream adoration:
                        This is the land of the free.
                        Scream 'til God hears you,
                        And all the rest fear you:
                        Tell them you heard it from me.

                                                              Oh, dearie, he
                                                              thinks he's a rebel!

[Oh, the I, ME, MINE of my poetic self-consumption!]

April buys me a Labatt's
and laughs at my poem.
                                                              Sure, she wonders
                                                              what in hell it's
                                                              supposed to mean.

                                                              Hush now! She loves
                                                              him! How sweeeet!

We sit in the back.
I look her in the eye
and see a new language
against "Uncle John's Band,"
decide to take
the ultimate risk,
and make form from
the sudden silence in the bar.

The Oswego Fugues

III

I see
her face reflect
in the TV screen
as my love sleeps
in the small room
on East Sixth,
car shadows walking
along warm walls,
and words again
falling into
my empty lap.

    As they walk the
    walls of West Eighth
    and Oneida.

Later, I read
her essay on beluga whales.
I've caught up
with her
and sit in St. Joe's
watching her kneel
and turn to cantos of prayer.

    He wonders:
    Is it Merton's
    burning song, or
    Dickinson's "fine
    invention"?[5]

The water is all water,
is flames on her forehead
as down the steps—one, two—
down these old steps of mine,
down these cracked, perfect steps—three, four.

    She doesn't know she
    has taken him back.

    Now, a *real* counting
    in the heart of the
    young versifier.

These steps, where I can see
the shoes, her plain
brown shoes, and think
of what I see here then:
That after death,
I'll follow the long line
of shoes walking, walking;

    Those years ago,
    a child in church.

    But how to tell them
    we walk into the
    light of ourselves?

Stephen Murabito

I will not lift up my eyes
to see this thing I think I know—

to trust the steadfast awe,
the light that draws us in:

> Oh, do not turn for me:
> I will be behind you;
> I will be the last
> in your great number

into the singularity of human echo.

It's a Wednesday,
sometime in early March.
Ontario still slings
its sleet in sheets,
and we find cover
under the post office overhang,
the ancient civic shade.

> Here, there's only
> ice, and no roses
> to climb the walls.

Beluga whales? I ask.
For zoology, she says.

And the shit
from the sky and lake
never stops her
into stories
about the world's oceans:

> Not of herself
> but always of
> the other, the
> passionate goal
> to serve inside
> of the student.

the Sally Lightfoot crab,
the Queen angelfish,
the Kergulen fur seal.

Despite all this, I only care about my next
beer. Yet I start to see the world
has spun a light inside her eyes,

> It's a sound
> deeper than
> reasoned belief.

and I wonder if I know her God,
the insights and appearances,
and I hear my Wallace Stevens.

> *Why when the singing ended and we turned*
> *Toward the town, tell why . . .*[6]

The Oswego Fugues

And so I do what I always do.
I write a poem on a paper bag:

                    Oh, goodie—
                    his early work
                    has such kick!

        A Cup in the Morning

        I had coffee and tea
        With Jesus Christ;
        By the time I got mine,
        It was cold as ice.

        I asked him, *Could you*
        Pass the cream, please?
        He said nothing,
        So I got on my knees.

        I prayed and prayed,
        And I prayed all day:
        I had never thought
        Of cream this way.

        I wondered if he
        Had the power,
        Or if the cream
        Would turn and sour.

        The next day, there came
        Some tea for two:
        I'll have mine black;
        How about you?

                    She laughs but
                    of course questions
                    his belief.

We move
in words
down to the warmth,
down to the Ferris Wheel,
where we sit
by the fire
by the window
by the whiteness
over the lake: It breaks to us
like another world
born beyond the windows
and Garcia's "Sugaree."

                    He hears an echo
                    telling him that he
                    will see it clearly,
                    that it will one day
                    break back to him.

Stephen Murabito

The next afternoon,
she meets me at
the Irish Inn.

I step into the song
of smoke and drink and talk.
But the sun that falls

against their faces—
it's not a thing
that we have made

but nonetheless
is pulse of sound
and human portal.

How can I name it?

The floor that haunts
with its millionth creak,
these men, their lives,
while outside, the trees—

> Oh, Mrs. Leary
> coming in for a quart
> of cold Genesee,
> the TV soaps have gone
> to hide in Kingsford
> Park.

> She worries the
> choice, reaching
> back, back for the
> blessed bottle. It
> sweats to life as
> she pulls it out.

> *Oh! Blessed rage for order . . .*

There's hope tapped in
fresh packs of smokes
as the light slides down

the mirrored bar.

> *And of ourselves and of our origins . . .*

The Oswego Fugues

The stilled mind
I long to join
can pierce this chaos,

this sealed thing.
But how to name
in 4/4 time

while Jimmy Dean's
"Merry Christmas, Peggy"
fills up the bar,

and Johnny Burke,
layed off a year,
takes Mrs. L.

to twirl in plumes,
and the jukebox
was never sweeter?

She asks what I think.   Someone requests K 11.

She asks again.   They say, Mum, you
I have the guts   just know when you're
to start to tell.   falling in love.

IV

And the next day
we walk the streets,
the brilliant Eastside streets
of Oswego, where children scream and play,
and from the shady alleyway
between two houses on Erie Street,   He knows it will
the ancient gardener steps out   happen, but she
stops, looks at us, and smiles,   is startled
runs the one long sleeve across   by the sudden face—
his glistening brown forehead,   oh, a face of faces.

Thosea damned tomatoes,
they nota grow right.
I donna know what the hell
I'ma gonna do with them!

Stephen Murabito

And on East Fifth, the world's
allegro con molto brio with life.
And somewhere in between
the streets, between the two of us,
between his story and the history of our people,
between who I am
and what this place sings out to me,
especially now that she—

I see her words.
They open,
receiving me.
She holds my hand,
and I fall through to her,
a simple movement
of sun and eye and shoe and voice and breath,
and the soft hand.
Oh, she,
a simple tumbling of words,
echoing flames that they become,
to make that day a day
to fire a soul to life
when we are now
between ourselves—
oh, she
begins to make.

V

From "Subject Profiles: Os-33 and Os-34" September, 1977

[A]nd we followed the two young men on the way to their bar (the Ferris Wheel). They improvised a song called "Heroin Pie." They took turns, one offering a couplet, and the other tallying back with a couplet, the entire exchange turning on alternate rhyming. It was windy, and we could not keep up with them, especially Os-34, who was the fastest walker any of us had ever seen, so we didn't get this particular song of theirs on tape.

The Oswego Fugues

When this spontaneous song had run its lyrical course, the two continued on toward the river and over the bridge, all the while whistling what appeared to be a fugue, each handling two "voices" in the exchange. This was by far the most frustrating observation for our research team. Before opening the door to the tavern, Os-33 turned to his friend and quoted from James Joyce's "Counterparts": "The barometer of his emotional nature was set for a spell of riot." Then laughing, he was into the bar. Os-34, more to the night, answered, "Of this much, we can be certain."

The following day, we asked Os-33 about the dialogue at the tavern door, and he produced Os-34's response exactly although he was clearly in the throng, and a band was playing when Os-34 gave his response.

Several of us were intrigued by Os-33's creative sensibilities. We decided to pose the following question to him:

> Yes, you're good with words; yes, you're a fast thinker;
> and yes, you seem to be a reasonably well-read young
> poet. However, what's your *purpose* with language;
> what's your ultimate critical and cultural mission?

We were surprised by his response or lack thereof. He genuinely seemed stumped by the question, and it was the first time that he asked any of us to repeat a thing we'd said. He then responded:

> I don't know . . . I guess I want to leave something
> lasting . . . I don't know. I'd like to be a thinker in
> an unthinking society, but that's not enough. I mean
> based on what you've asked me, that's just what *I'd*
> like to be, not what my work needs to be. So, I guess I
> don't know . . . But I think I can find that—what you're
> talking about—if I just keep exploring the continuum
> of form and possibility. I guess it's somewhere
> between the degrees of that. I know I'd like to go to
> graduate school—maybe Iowa, maybe Pitt. I don't
> know . . . I get the idea that something will break to me.

Stephen Murabito

Then,
some controlled implosion.
      Oh! Blessed rage . . .

And now,
the voices words need to embrace.
      Blessed rage for order, pale Ramon, . . .

That my voice can show their lives.
      And of ourselves, and of our origins . . .

Now, back home, alone
on the black night water,
I strip down
and wade in.

Here the coldness
simply waits out the seasons,
a patience, never leaving,
like some echo inside the stones underfoot,
and there's nothing romantic about it,
down to the changing aquifer,
except the lessons earth teaches.

But still this coldness waits
to be wind or snow or driving rain,
a music in the voiceless world.

I come back home
to walk up Polish Hill
and talk to the old folks
and fall in love
with their inaccurate stories
and still more, their loving memories
as they rename themselves
through history, love, and invention:
The place like every lived-place,
remakes itself via people
so certain that they can recall
what never may have happened.[7]

The Oswego Fugues

I come to hope
the words will run through me.
But I go where
I can close my eyes
and wade through great lake waves,
to the deep, to the black,
as the water
closes around me
like shouting
gone silent
to echo.

VI
Ode to Bach's *The Art of the Fugue*
(for Thaddeus Iorizzo)

> Bach was not a harmonist for whom the
> vertical homophony had prime importance:
> he was a composer of counterpoint, i.e., of
> horizontal voices, each of equal importance,
> which were bound together by the most artful
> structural devices. [. . .] Bach devoted the rest of
> his life to this idea, knowing that he would
> reach here the climax of his art. He knew that
> the trend of the period had turned against him
> and had isolated him.
> Edward Cole[8]

> When thou art with me
> I walk in joy
> To meet eternal peace.
> Oh, how cheerfully content
> Were thus my end
> When my loyal eyes
> Be closed by thy fair hand.
> J. S. Bach[9]

> It is by their syllables that words juxtapose
> in beauty, by these particles of sound as clearly
> as by the sense of the words which they compose.
>
> Charles Olson[10]

Stephen Murabito

This irony, though,

                        a man
                        hearing it all

                        should be alone
                        in his time,

                                                                These fugues,
                                                                his life's work,
                                                                his final notes,
                                                                his last songs of
                                                                voices of life.

a singularity
from stillness
born of striving movement.

Suddenly this:
                        four voices,
                        metamorphic extension,
                        inversion,
                        polyphonic transition.

                                                                And from these
                                                               pieces: *From* them
                                                               something like a
                                                               world will be
                                                               discovered . . .[11]

Bass,
tenor,
alto, soprano:
a singularity,
a rootwork of water on glass;

lines
opening
rain down long windows,
with branches, bark lines
closing.

This suddenly:
                        upward from every angle,
                        lives in sixteenth notes
                        to chromatic perfection
                        opening lines.

                                                                The unfolding, the
                                                               repetition, the
                                                               variation of lives at
                                                               allegro con brio, of
                                                               our voices *tutti,*
                                                               stretto maestrale.[12]

The Oswego Fugues

But yet one: I am here,
here through all voices,
at all points beside you,
around you,
part of you
becoming you
as it moves on,
as we move on,
hearing it all.
You are alone
yet with me.

                                                                            We're voices
                                                                            crossing
                                                                            yet always aligned—
                                                                            Contrapuncti I-XIV,
                                                                            human *Fugen.*

Statement/theme;
inversion/reversal:
                    Our steps
                    what we make of ourselves
                    of ourselves and of our origins . . .
                    crossing
                    from stillness to story.

Oh, suddenly this:
hearing an extension,
polyphonic rain
closes over us,
and we aren't alone
though all angles
surround us,

                                          Then and now fuse
                                          to a portal in place,
                                          where living and dead
                                          are one light of mind.

                    and we cross
                    to align,
                    fugues of human act,

reversing inversions,
ourselves making
what our steps become,
what steps become our theme.

Stephen Murabito

>   Alto, soprano, tenor,
>   bass—time marked
>   here: a singularity
>   turning plural, a
>   thread to threads
>   in changing contexts
>   yet always traceable.

Back to
inversion/theme
reversal/statement—
crossing voices.

We're the answer
born inside all
those questions:
          a man,
          a woman,
          ironies
          extending
          polyphonically.

Moving, we move
mind, heart, soul,
no pause
just lived-silence,

a turning back,
          between notes where
          knowledge reverberates,
          and voices break back to us,
and we see
and hear
everything
there could be

on all sides
of the echoes
we come to embrace.

The Oswego Fugues

Fugue Four:

The Wonderful Chaos

The Oswego Fugues

Stephen Murabito

I

        Syllabus

You will teach me, first, my students,
the character of my indifference,
and the dark confusion of being young;
I will teach you, then, my students,
the hope that lies beneath the surface,
a love inherent in the nature of things.
Follow the course of it to the end of knowing;
gather the thread of it line by line.

        Michael True[1]

After screaming too many poems
into the lake wind and failing
out of college, I return
to sit in the dark lobby,
on the leathered bench

and gaze
up at the painting
of Edward Austin Sheldon,[2]
benevolent pedagogue,
circa 1891,
white beard,
shaved upper lip.

Look, Mum, he's found
a comfy spot for such
deep contemplations.

Hush, he's learning;
he's starting to see.

A funkiness from
another time, cool
to the young
man eager to return,
try it again:[3]
People believe in
him this time, and he
burns with wanting
connections to cohere.

Professor Sheldon, you smile
and look forever instructive,
lips ready to speak, to ask
your burning
teacher's question.

There is a universal
light within it.

The Oswego Fugues

    And your teachers—their faces
    are sterner than ours, yet there
    are those same giving eyes,
    those same desires to listen.

    I hold my *Divine Comedy*,
    sweat tight at its worn binding,
    and I see the empty corridors
    flood with spirits wrapped   He sees it,
    in the threads of promise,   *the thread of it*.[4]
    the layers
    of this learning and discovery,   Can it be his?
    the mindful purpose,
    eternal heat
    received and passed,
    that forever strain and human weave.
            [Text: (ME, fr. OFr. *texte*, fr. L
            textus, fabric, structure,
            fr. *textus*, pp. of *texere,* to weave);[5]
            noun from verb,
            thing from act,
            unending process,
            action/reaction.]

    My first day back on this campus
    after two years of searching,

    I come from Turco's workshop class
    and wait for Cinoti's World Lit.

    I sit and smoke and see a pulse,   But he can't
    the *hope that lies beneath the surface*.   quite name it then.

    Oswego State, I say   The hillside college
    of my new home,   on the lakeshore.

    and feel my soul begin to live
    in this connective condition: The vague, beautiful
                                                         swirling lasts forever.
    ideas, family, histories,
    the threads and layers,
                  a love inherent in the nature of things,
        fragmented shafts of light
        through the ancient lobby windows.

Stephen Murabito

II

There is a longer ladder yet to climb:
This much is not enough,[6] she reads, her hand raised

as, echoing, that part of *The Inferno*
is the night's reading and discussion.

Suddenly, words never mean more to me,
and I blab on and on about

how we are like Dante, falling and rising.
I'd better stop: I'm not making sense, I say.

You've made connections, though, she says,
and that's always the start of sense.

I feel that rush as her back is turned,
and she writes on the board, quoting Henry James:

To criticise is to appreciate, to appropriate,
to take intellectual possession,

to establish in fine a relation with
the criticised thing and make it one's own.[7]

You'd better plan on taking possession.
You'd better plan on making it your own,

she says, *especially if you want careers*
in the humanities, where it is

rung on rung of Dante's ladder
with splinters through your thin shoes.

We discuss the *it*, the struggle, the strife,
the claiming. She loves the *exfoliating*

terza rima, which mirrors Dante's mind:
And the pulse is the pulse of learning.

The Oswego Fugues

We spend the rest in good connections,
startled at what readers we've become.

We move back through the cantos and point,
our fingers moving all through the text.

Then Rossi, with his Herbert, quotes, "Strive in this,
and love the strife" from "The Banquet."[8]

In fact, he carries the book with him. Oh, I see
my friend: Rossi, who beams with life and thinks

that everything begins in words, who thinks it all
is sayable, that words have lost nothing across time;

Rossi, who writes these long romantic poems;
Rossi, who never *comes* to words or *uses* words;

Rossi, who *lives* in words, is somehow *born* there;
Rossi: arms waving, face blood red; Rossi: consumed.

We get back to the *it*, Dante's struggle and his ardor,
and our possessive claiming, and by then we're laughing.

She says, *Take it with you; fashion it; perfect it.*

To think	To this day,	
she explains	he can still see her	
Dante for hours,	smiling up	
and in that time	from those books	voices
the great poet	that one night,	
breaks back	Oswego bitter cold.	
to her	Oh, they remain	
and then, of course,	open on her desk	
to us.	as he turns to leave.	

Stephen Murabito

III

Oh, Rossi, who becomes my friend;
Rossi, who writes like Donne, Coleridge, and Keats;

Oh, Rossi, who goes on to teach
his English for twelve years in Syracuse;

Oh, Rossi, whose words spiral up
between our worlds; Rossi, who

is dying now, sends me this tape,
somehow the voice still resilient:

> *. . . And it hit me, Joey,*
> *one day in Physical Therapy*
> *as I stared ahead*
> *at the wonderful curtain*
> *between us all,*
> *you know, with those*
> *pastel patches I wrote you about*
> *shaped like all the states,*
> *places I'll never make it to:*
>
> *It hit me*
> *what I'd say*
> *to the kids.*
>
> *So the next day, man,*
> *Bonnie and little Woodie,*
> *I told them*
> *that I wasn't*
> *going to get any better,*
> *that it was like*
> *when Mommy went to see God*
> *after her car accident,*
> *but that this time*
> *I needed*
> *to be their baby,*
> *that that's what death was,*
> *that they needed to hold me*
> *and just be with me,*
> *that I was their baby.*

The Oswego Fugues

>*And, boy, I lost it.*
>*I swore that I wasn't gonna*
>*do that, that I'd be strong.*
>*But I lost it*
>*when Woodie held my leg,*
>*and Bonnie,*
>*like she always did,*
>*started climbing my body*
>*to her place.*
>
>*Man, her strength,*
>*those small powerful hands:*
>*Her sheer strength blew me away.*
>*My neck just went limp,*
>*and that's what it means to die, man:*
>*Parts of your body*
>*just releasing themselves*
>*to sudden greater strengths*
>*that come out of nowhere:*
>*That's what* hope *and* answer *mean, too.*
>
>*But I released myself to her,*
>*a four year-old child*
>*with the natural strength*
>*to obliterate pain,*
>*to make all the needles*
>*and probes and human futility*
>*disappear.*
>*I'm tellin' ya, my heart broke*
>*and blossomed*
>*at the same time.*
>
>*That's what death is, too,*
>*Joey, that breaking-blossoming*
>*when your three year-old son*
>*says,* You don't have to cry, Daddy,
>*not* Don't cry,
>*or* Why are you crying?
>*I mean, there's this intuitive forgiveness,*
>*this thing he can't possibly know*
>*he's saying to me.*
>*And I told them*
>*that that's what death was, too,*
>*not only forgiving someone*
>*who just can't fight any more,*
>*but loving him or her for it.*

Stephen Murabito

And no shit, Joey,
Bonnie—and she looked
so much like Nancy
my chest ached—
Bonnie asked if death
were like liking
someone a whole lot
(a whole lot—
she's been saying that
since before Nan died).

But I realized then
as I looked past those
broad, dark cheeks
and into her brown eyes
that she was such a big girl,
and I had this flash
just for a second
of what she'll look like
in twenty years,
how nice and sweet she'll be.

But she was this child
and this little girl
at the same time,
such an alive thing herself.

And she had that look
we all get
when we make
a great connection.
It's no fucking wonder
Joyce gets the word epiphany
from religion.
It's just no fucking wonder
I could hardly speak.
And that fucking
unpronounceable drug
dried my mouth out
so much I had to laugh
because I remembered
smoking all that dope
with you and Ronnie
when he got all that
African shit—remember
how we couldn't drink
enough beer or catch our breath?

The Oswego Fugues

But I told Bonnie,
Yeah, death is
really the same as love,
but you have to let go,
and you can get mad
at the world
but not at the person.

Woodie, hell, he was on the floor
and ripping into some donated magazine.
I don't even remember
when he stopped holding my leg.

And that's what it is, too, man,
this loss of all sense of time
and boundary,
even with simple stuff like that.

But I could tell that Bonnie
was really trying
to get what I was saying,
that she was using
every last thing she had
and then some.
And I felt this pang of pity
that I never felt for any student
but maybe should have—
you know, that he or she
was bringing everything to bear
on whatever god-awful text
I asked him or her to read.

You know, students are
the most beautiful
while they're taking finals.
I used to watch them,
their faces stern and alive
with thinking—what human grace,
all of that struggle in one room.

Stephen Murabito

*But Bonnie's face,
it mirrored for me
how hard I tried
to understand* The Paradiso
in Cinoti's class,[9]
*how I got an A
on that final paper
she made me write
about Herbert and Dante.
Remember? Didn't you
proofread the damned thing?*

*Man, when I went to see her
after she gave me the assignment,
she said there were parts
of Dante that she never understood
completely, parts that would
only become clear if she looked
and looked again right through them,
that their meaning would break
to her. She said she read
and reread some parts of* Paradiso
*thirty times.
Man, that blew me away.
Coming out of her office,
I felt bathed not just in confidence,
but in a kind of knowing,
a kind of being.
And I knew I'd spend my life teaching.*

*I mean, Cinoti called my paper
a living struggle to connect
and said it was about difficulty
itself, a demonstration of it.
And she said she learned from it,
that I taught her.
Imagine that:
I taught her.*

*And that's death, too,
this sudden remembering
how huge the little
things were along the way.*

The Oswego Fugues

*And Bonnie got that squint,
that flush
she gets from Nancy,
and that little tilt
of her head
she gets from me.*

*But, Joey,
that was it;
there wasn't any going
beyond that.
She understood all she could.
She opened herself up
as much as possible.
I kept telling myself
that I was there,
at least I was there
to see that opening.*

*One second she was
the flesh and blood
of every question Nancy
and I ever asked,
and the next second
she was off playing
with Woodie on the floor
until their Aunt Gina
came and got them.*

*That was yesterday.
I sat there for a bit
in the greatest peace
I'd ever known,
and my heart and body
finally stopped aching,
and I wanted to die.*

I've accepted it.

*And that's death, too.
That's the irony
that literature doesn't always teach:
Sometimes, you wanna die.
Everything's right.
Everything's all right.*

Stephen Murabito

*Then there were four pills
I was being told to swallow.
And they made me try to eat
something looking like piss.*

*And I thought of how earthbound
we really are.*

*Some fucker down the hall
was screaming about rigatoni.
He was bitching,
I don't want rigatoni!
How many times do
I have to tell you?!
The nurses were howling:
They weren't even giving
him rigatoni at all.
And somehow, I thought about you,
you and those food poems:
Let Bernardo write some
celebration of make-believe
rigatoni, I thought.*

*Anyway, I've said too much—
I'm gettin' tired . . .
These drugs make it go away . . .
But only for a little while . . .
Joey, the kids
will be with Gina . . .
You know, her and Dale
are . . . great people . . .
Oh . . . shit . . .*

He is weeping

I don't want

Don't worry, man

my voice to fade away.

I'll hear it again

Once in a while

You live in words

if you see them,

Every time I look

Bonnie and Woodie,

I'll see you there

Joey, tell them

Your passionate strife

something about me.

The Oswego Fugues

IV

Dr. Harbert,[10]
in the fall of 1979,
gives us the philosophy final
without a question.

Of course, it is
Metaphysics—
the blue books coming around,
his patience present

in this simple act:
Write what you know.
No awkward questions
to trip us into

what we don't know.
Johnny Hogan—studying
to be a priest—
jokes, *I quess there's*

no cheating then, huh?
And we all laugh.

I spend two hours
with pens unrolling
word after word
to get to definitions,

                      He hopes like hell
                      a term's knowledge
                      will break back
                      in fluid words.

insights. I write toward
a metaphysical knowledge,
see lived-moments
of lake or farm.
                      But not a church pew.

I follow words
down their corridors,
am a yearning, perhaps
a face of the grace Rossi sees.

                      We can only imagine
                      what Dr. Harbert sees
                      in those beautiful,
                      flushed faces.

Stephen Murabito

And lesson two: It comes back
to you. Those yellowed words
will sit down across the table,
and you will see yourself

just as you are when you
first tell yourself *think, think:*
Explain who we are.
Discover a root metaphor.

It will sit down beside you,
and you will regard it
as idea's sweet blues,
a sigh of human breath,

the thing that takes us, pulls
us up to where we thought we'd be,
and it returns us, too,
as it must be, be these things.

You will hold it gently,
not let it go, not toss it,
but turn to meet your teacher,
who can break back to you.

And when you rise to leave,
oh, sweet words of all we have
or have let slip through our hands,
it will get up and leave with you.

In/through that scribbled
text.

On a Saturday
morning, as he moves,
he pulls the blue book
from a dusty shelf—
it's been twenty
years.

The pages stiff,
cracking, but the
words resilient.

Ascending the cellar
steps, he carries a
box of books, the old
essay on top.

V

I fear the essay
without a question.

But I know that
mindless facts
will stay just that.

I have a smoke
and write a poem:

But back then, squinting at
the ungodly syntax of
philosophy,
he pulls an all-nighter
in Penfield's twenty-four-
hour room. He watches a
group of students attacking
each other with facts for
hours. Theirs will be a
multiple-choice final exam.

The Oswego Fugues

                The All-Nighter

                The all-nighter: It's here; it's here!
                We brought food, coffee, smokes, and beer.

                Let's study until our brains fall out,
                Ingest it all, get smart-boy's gout.

                Then we'll throw it up on the page
                And make the prof eat his own rage:

                He'll be shocked by the A's we got,
                Holding in his hands what we forgot.

I close my books
and go to look
for Fred or Jack or Claude
or Jimmy or Egger.
But no one is home,
just a pure darkness
in those streets,
so I sit on the porch.

Man, it must be three AM
at 18 West Fifth Street.
I look across
the line of dark houses

and see lights on at Chip's,
where he is up painting
his term projects.
I smoke one more,
with shadowy Heidegger.

I start down those steps
at least three times
but each time return to watch
my friend in all his passion

of color, vision, and brush-work.

This against the night
his high-school friends
are stoned on the
floor while he plays
piano: They listen to
soft Chopin leaving to
return again in
the improvisation.
They sleep. There is
the quietness of his
belonging to the air.
His girlfriend sits
on the bench: *That's
beautiful; play more.*
But he takes her hand
and drives her home.

Stephen Murabito

VI
(In Memory of Fred Bishop, 1945-1991)

Fred:

If I could find the words,
I'd thank you for your ideas,
your attention at our taverns
to the very syllable,
the sound, the thought,
the reason.

Oh, that rockface

(man, the dialectic
of black 'n' tans),

referentiality.

But I can't speak.
No words will come.

April tells me, *Honey, Fred Bishop died.*
and I keep waiting
for her to say
that it's a joke.

Your death leaves me stupid,
our dialogues falling through my fingers,
the silence taking root
at my feet.
And I've got to go teach.

Oh, I could stand there,
arms down,
looking stupid,
my mouth agape,
in this stunned silence,
and the words could fall
one at a time
like birds discovering flight,
clumsy and awkward,
an incomplete response.

And my students
could stare like kids
who crane their necks
up to those trees,
where this absurdity
ensues, confused
yet colorful,
their patience
suspended because

The Oswego Fugues

today's the *last* day of class,
and I have jokingly promised
a final class called
"What It All Means."

                    And English
                          composition
                                could come loose,
                  these standards
            and rules,
         these
            expectations
       and devices,
  unable to hold
  the chaos
from breaking.

And I could discuss
the superficial smoke and mirror
of order
and the wonder
of embracing this chaos.   Where a friend shows up
                                                    at your wedding with a
                                                    saucepan on his head;
                                                    where a friend is at the
                                                    bow of a rowboat firing toy
                                                    arrows at a ship docked in
                                                    the Port of Oswego.

Oswego:
I could simply say,
Oswego,
and let them wonder
at the single word.

Oswego:
I could say my word,
Oswego,
slowly like all water,
burning like olive eyes,
sweet like cigar smoke.

Stephen Murabito

Oswego:
Never a confusion,
but round,
circular,
a return
to the Wheel
or Lil's
or Larry's

or The Patch
or The Clam Bar
or The Irish Inn.

Oswego:
I could say it
as sweetly as possible
until my breath was spent,
and I could empty
my lungs numb
with story on story
and at last imagine.

Oswego:
I'd say it
because that's where
you are,
and where I want
to be—

back there,
where the words
are now one last
ironic joke.

You were no true
believer, yet
the preacher
tries his best.

Oswego:
And my students,
those who might remain,
would be absorbed
into my music,
into whatever's left,

A breaking back.
Everything can
be transmitted
in one word.

But still, not
a church pew.

I love this! Look, Mum!
The preacher eulogizes
the atheist, and all the fellas
are in their Hawaiian
shirts! They're bright as
parrots! Why,
antimourners is what they
are! What a stroke, a last
line in life's dialectic!

The Oswego Fugues

   and then we all
   might disappear
   into what it all really *does* mean

              [Language
                 (any kind), a
              thinking,
                      a connecting,
                 a return],
   into the wonderful chaos.

                                             Look! Turkey gizzards on
                                           his windowsill say, *Come
                                           out and fish for carp at
                                           four AM and live to watch the
                                           sun come up like another
                                           Socratic question behind
                                           the river, echoes
                                           of Plato and Ovid still
                                           ringing against one last
                                           smoke.* Come on, Joey, get
                                           your bloody pole and get
                                           out there!

                                           Oh, all this against

  the constant
  life as
  rising action,
  a metamorphosis
  with Genny Cream on draft,
       oh, the amber to brown
          to the swirling black
              of the Guiness Stout

           poured in . . .   Lil laughs behind the bar.
  a metamorphosis
   that starts with just a word
    then a question,
      then one answer
        from one of us,
     one possibility   This drinking and talking.
  on a continuum of connections   It's a social *mission,*
  on a continuum of eternal sense.   if you will.

Stephen Murabito

Oswego:
Fred,
it is our home.

What's the word mean, Mum?

Iroquois: *place where
the waters pour out.*[11]

But look at them: They
actually have books in
a bar on a Friday night!

You once tell me
that you would wish to die at school,
the hill of Syracuse University,

   a classroom,
   winter term,
   steam hissing,
   white chalkdust,

*There shall be commerce
between earth and Heaven—
the steeple aspires over the cobbles,
ringing the changes on bell, brick, and candle.*[12]

   that it is
   the best place
   in the world,
   and it is.

I have to go there now
to keep this thing
from dying.

Where we teach one
another about humor and
intellectual play.

Where I see you like
the living spark
between the halves of metaphor.

Where perhaps something
we do somehow filters
down to odd, unforeseen,
new contexts, finds new
homes, lives where all
converges and is kept
vital, deep in memory.

The Oswego Fugues

    Where from such wonderful
    chaos something more
    than wonder might emerge.

                                                Where first lines are born.

Where final lines break back and never die.

Fugue Five:

Young Lovers Stand There Against St. Stephen's

The Oswego Fugues

Stephen Murabito

> . . . Oh, gently, gently,
> do in love for him each day some reliable task, — lead him
> near to the garden, give him the heavy
> weight of night . . . . .
> Don't let him go . . . . .
>
> Rainer Maria Rilke
> *Duino Elegy Number Three*[1]

I

I go back to Eighth Street,
back to move alone and see
the place holding on:

    Mrs. Pinelli sits
    in her breezeway.

To seek out: This is
the very beginning.

Oh, he plays there,
the rose garden gone,
his first beer there,
a piss-warm Utica Club
with Paulie D., spit-out,
foaming laughter, a brown
bottle, blazing glass by
her brilliant azaleas,
and they're gone now,
too. But she comes out
and howls her very
life into his face, and
the boys split up.
Oneida, Mohawk, Seventh,
Eighth, just names his
feet fly over in a fugue,
in this running away.

In '64, I run away,
six miles in my mind—
all the way to Ninth and Utica,

The Oswego Fugues

into another world,
my father pulling up
in the '56 Chevy,

the window down,

> *Come on, sport,*
> *get in. I know how it is.*
> *The world's just too big*
>
> *for you now, is all.*
> *Come on, Joey, you can help*
> *me put up the candy aisle.*

Mrs. Pinelli
sits in her breezeway.
I pass and look.

Then she looks up,
and I wave,
and she smiles
but doesn't know me.

On Seventh, Mr. Kazinsky
sits on his porch,
the white head flung back.

It is a Friday afternoon
in warm and heavy June;
his wife and kids are gone now, too:

Pretending he is
running groceries,
the boy stands on
the front seat and
turns and turns
the steering wheel.

Her gaze, a sadness,
is off to one side
of her magazine
as if the words have
spilled over the edge.

Oh, these streets turn
and turn in his mind.
They break back.
He'll never transcend
them.

Louisiana, Arizona,
places ring in the poet's
mind like states of
being.

Stephen Murabito

Oh, this, yes, this
is measured out:
West Eighth and Oneida,
to Seventh and Mohawk,
the angles cut
through voices and
geography.

We talk.
Mr. Kaz says,

> *Joey, she*
> *died in '87.*

Johnny King says,

> *The last time I*
> *moved through this place,*
> *what struck me was*
> *it was Wednesday, Joey.*
> *Wednesday! And not a smell*
> *of sauce anywhere,*
> *not even over*
> *at old man Rizzo's.*

I see
the young man
moving into
the disappearing landscape,
the young man
running further
than Ninth and Utica.

He chases Vivvie by
that old mailbox.
She gets away,
giggling the world
into snowfall.

He sits and draws
breath over there
on that small curb.

And the fresh fish
display coolers
down at Cahill's
are gone now, too.
But his fish sandwich
there is sweet, sweeter
still in the river air,
breathed in salty,
breathed in and sung back
by the incantatory gulls.

The Oswego Fugues

                                        There, across the tracks
                                        beyond Vona's Restaurant.
                                        If we hurry, we can—no.

Now, I walk through it,
ascend Polish Hill
step on step, not knowing why—
Hawley to Tallman,
Niagara to Verrick
to Ellen, to Erie, to Hart.[2]

Young lovers stand there   Her tan leg curls around
against St. Stephen's Church: his calf as if they can
Oh, I see their radiance.   transcend mortality.

II

I see   But most of all,
Mr. Zicci   the poet has returned
up on Eighth Street,   to seek the old woman:
where he cut wild roses   Just to see her, just
for his wife,   to speak with her,
cut them with his   maybe that will—
aged and pained hands.

        They grew over the edge
        of the garage out back.
        Joey, they'd come, over the years,
        to crawl all the way
        over ta the one side.
        She'd gone blind, but still
        she could touch 'em, tell me where
        the damned things needed to be trimmed.
        Ah, them nights when the roses
        were up against the windowpanes,
        and you could smell 'em on the breeze.

Moving slowly,
they went for walks,
her with the cane
he now holds
caged in his fingers
after offering a beer:

Stephen Murabito

That cane's an antique.
She got it from
her Aunt Marie,
and she got it
from her mother:
She knew a man
down the Sinclair
Chair Company
in old Oswego.
He made canes on the side.

And after a pause, the smile,
Every day, Joey,
every day, we went about this time.

He hands it to me
to hold through his story
but against his words,

I see them move,   Down Oneida, up to Ninth,
but I can't hear   over to Mohawk, these the
a word they say.   lit steps of their time.

III

Ah, ya better not go, kiddo.   The poet has asked if
She's had another stroke.   he can go visit her
She rambles now, Joey.   in the nursing home.
She don't know nobody.
Sometimes, not even me.
Try to understand, he says
as he takes back the cane.
                                       But he goes anyway.

Her voice begins to break
in the dull, sunny driveway:
Visitor Parking,
Saint Luke's Home,
Saint Luke's Chapel,
saints, names, and faces and statues.

The Oswego Fugues

                                            And as he parks his car
                                            and closes his eyes, oh,
                                            there she is—in a
                                            hallway chair, face a
                                            horror unsayable, eyes
                                            exploded glass, hands up,
                                            up in praise and fear,
                                            fingers old roots of
                                            flesh poised in the air.

I hear
Mrs. Zicci,
her voice in my soul.

She's telling the doctor,
the sudden hallway doctor,
        Isa no good. No life.
She bites out   This pained, patient
her thick Italian,   listening against when
        I tella you, give me   he is arrested, wails
        somma pill—I wanna   in Cell Number Three on his blues
        finish all dis torture.   harp. He opens his
        My eyesa see too much.   eyes; the sudden cop
                                         says, *It's ok: Play!*
I make it to the lobby,   He turns to the wall
but the smell, the smell   but then slowly plays.
the smell of urine, of rotting flesh.

        The doctor jokes, *You can't*
        do that. I've got a lot of
        money yet to make from
        you, sweetheart!

But she is ninety-nine,
eyes gone
to pits   She's returned to Sicily,
behind thick frames.   Provincia di Catania.

Then wheels, the wheels,
the wheels: Here comes
the medicine
for dead legs,
for numb feet—
the gift of slippers
will be useless.

Stephen Murabito

Lost legs,
lost house,
lost bank.
No money,
no nothing.

I hear her scream,
    Oh, where
        are my hands?

And then she speaks
in Sicilian tongues.

Mrs. Zicci sings sweetly,
her eyes closed, her head up.

Then all other voices disappear
into the sudden flatness
of her grave cry,

    na, na, na, ma;
    na, na, na, ma.

But this, this is
not music, not—we
are just two souls in wait.

The doctor walks away,
is now lives away.

He sits near her,
lowers his head, weeps.

Oh, *stretto,*
stretto maestrale,[3]
the voices surround them.

He knows she speaks to
him; he knows she sees
him there, has for days.

IV

Three beers in
Papa says,

    Joey, ya know
    Jasper died
    playin' pitch
    down the Elks.
    That's the way
    to go, man!
    Friends, a cold one,
    a good hand the last
    thing ya see!

The Oswego Fugues

                                            The face changes:
                                            Oh, a certain
                                            knowledge in its lines
                                            but nothing like her
                                            symphony turned black.

                  None of this
                  nursin' home
                  shit! Jesus
                  Christ, the pills.
                  You'd never
                  better put
                  me in there.
                  Some stranger
                  wipes your ass!
                  That ain't no way to live.

Okay, I promise, *okay.*

We laugh,
but I am still
blinded
by what I heard,
and all that I can think
to do is walk the streets
of town and then perhaps
out to the lake.

V

                                        Stay for me there: I will not faile
                                          To meet Thee in that hollow Vale.
                                          And think not much of my delay;
                                          I am already on the way,
                                          And follow Thee with all the speed
                                          Desires can make or Sorrowes breed.

                                                           Bishop Henry King
                                                           "An Exequy"[4]

Mr. Z.'s eye catching itself

in the sideview mirror

of his parked, meaningless Ford LTD.

Stephen Murabito

Eight Street, Eighth Street, Eighth Street:

tomato stakes in a heap,
green grass
and brown sticks
aged with old earth,
patch of untilled soil,
a bike wheel in a yard.

An inexorable human weight,
body in a breezeway,
eyes lifting out a window.

Sun yelling down one last alleyway,

robin feathers on an old onion crate.

A garage
door shuts
like a tomb.

Steps in a house,
movements to a drawer—
closer, closer,
photo of her by the '38 Buick.

Her smile, the red lipstick,
the gold cross at her throat,
the long white cotton dress.

She *is* beautiful,
a highball held up.

Up steps now, our endless steps.

These are
shapes and colors,
but the textures
have lost their voices.
He sees a postponed
promise to a grandson.

There is no language.

The roses are falling
into the shade now.

Back there, in '39, she
cleans a string of
trout, gagging for an
hour. God, look, see how
they laugh, fry it,
eat it with coleslaw, and
then drink cold Genesee.

It is a blossoming,
a rounded, gleaming
thing—an emergence.

Life, life in the flesh.

Mr. Z. will ascend,
the stairs, the climb,
the body left behind.

The Oswego Fugues

Black shoes on red carpet,
a hand on a railing,
then on a doorknob;
a hand over hangers,
an empty hand over dresses,

the last step deeper into the closet.

Gently, that cotton dress.   He promises he won't,
She hasn't worn it in years.   but he can't help it:
Oh, the fragrant essence.   Just the one inhalation.
          And she breaks back to him.

I see Mr. Zicci
take down the wooden chair,
down from its rusted hook
on the garage wall,
down and unfold it,
and sit, then slump.
He holds a tackle box
in his arms.

He rocks it like a child.

VI

> They came there regularly every evening drawn by some
> need. It was as if the water floated off and set sailing thoughts
> which had grown stagnant on dry land, and gave to their bodies
> even some sort of physical relief.
>
>   Virginia Woolf
>   *To the Lighthouse*[5]

    Here, one sits   Oh, the Oswego sunset,
for hours   and every voice
and, try to imagine,   behind it.
comes to believe
even if only hypnotized by waves,
that everything is divisible
out to a deep simplicity
and breathing tranquility,

Stephen Murabito

      comes to believe
that, in a sense,
over driftwood, stone, rock,
through clear green shallows,
out to the line of deeper blue,
he is at more than a land's edge
as the clouds obscure the horizonline
that late summer night
when the lake wind picks up,
and the fishing boats move in,

      yes, comes to believe
he is at an edge,
that the land
could give way,
becoming divisible, dissoluble,
turning dialogue to monologue
to one man left speechless
without geography or language,
the water reclaiming everything—
place, even dream of place,
and loved human faces, too.

      Here, worlds
merge from known
and unknowable voices,
their human trembling
behind one's back,
and streets and names,
like music,
oh, histories and flesh,
may turn every
lakeside, early evening inhalation
into the silver purity
of the quiet time passing,
and wave upon red wave
returning like one breath,
to flow out again.

The Oswego Fugues

      And slowly,
one comes to know,
with the intuitive certainty
that is the true weight of place,
why the angler,
just out there,
sets down her pole
and sits in her small boat
for the time it takes
the sun to set—

oh, the rest
of the sun to set.

Fugue Six:

The Greater Telling

The Oswego Fugues

Stephen Murabito

> Yet, behind the sound
> of trees is another
> sound. Sometimes, lying
> awake, or standing
> like this in the yard, I hear it. It
> ties our human telling
> to its course
> by momentum, and ours
> is merely part
> of its unbroken
> stream, the human
> and otherwise simultaneously
> told. The past
> doesn't fall away, the past
> joins the greater
> telling, and is.
>
> Li-Young Lee
> "Furious Versions"[1]

> Sing us, they say,
> a song you remember . . .
>
> Kathleen Norris
> "What Song, Then?"[2]

I

These words refer to   Oh, he will join
                                          their voices.

          their lives on padded kneelers.
          Outside it snows.
          The old folks are thinking of snow.
          It darkens stained-glass windows.
          It will surround them.
          They are in their kitchens
          against these puddles on grey marble.
          Some can see the docks
          from their Eastside windows.
          The water where river
          meets lake has turned black in the wind.

The Oswego Fugues

I see,
see hearts in the grain
of wooden pews.

          Theirs are the wrists
          that stop shaking when the palms
          surround a bowl of minestrone,
          the aroma of Romano rising, rising.

                    In the choir, years ago,
                    Anna Corradino, Jean
                    Salesi, Father Filomeno
                    Geremia . . . There's Nancy
                    LaFortuna Bernardo
                    pausing in her quiet
                    sewing room that
                    first winter day after
                    Joe passes on: Stitch by
                    stitch, she moves through
                    her sorrow, stopping,
                    thinking she'll *never let*
                    him go.[3]

                    This—he sees *this* in one
                    pulse of burning sense.

She is a tired seamstress now,
and she wonders if anyone
will tell her story:
In the early days on the farm,
they are harvesting a life
from the sweet soil of Scriba,
green onion shoots in spring,
the heavy iceburg in June,
all winter sewing onion bags—   All fall and winter,
the smell, it never washes away;   she sews clothes,
that life never washes away.   makes the *pasta e fasuli,*
But her Joe, a broad smile,   stirring in the shells,
hands nearly dark as baking earth   smiling at navy beans,
some hot July in Oswego.   thinking the fresh bread
                                                will be nice, will be.

Stephen Murabito

II

These words refer to
>their tired, aching bodies,
>laced against the holy blue columns.
>They sit, break bread, pour "Dago Red,"
>and live to tell about coming
>over from the old country.
>Grandpa feels his knees wobble
>with the overwhelming possibility
>of being American as he stands
>on Ellis Island and says who he is
>to impatient and uniformed strangers,
>one of whom wants to rename him.
>He refuses, refuses, and almost
>gets arrested. He takes the pen,
>the bastard's pen, and then perfectly
>spells out *Giuseppe Sebastiano Bernardo*.
>There are tears in his eyes.

I see them all
move in their old clothes
as they search out
the houses of their future.

His name survives, rings
out on the keys of an
Ellis Island typewriter.

I *know:* I see
their faces at the docks.
Their hands hold scraps of paper.

Dreaming of farmland,
he comes to Oswego,
address in hand.

It makes no sense then,
in a small church,
the old woman holding me.

How do you name having
seen human desire?
You howl in flesh's cage.

These words refer to
>their backs, flesh angling down, down
>against the curtain of the back confessional
>as they weed-out the earth to a brown perfection,
>as they gather stones like small change
>onto the trucks or piles along the muck beds.
>I marvel at Grandma's hands
>(like they have minds of their own),
>marvel how they pick the weeds away,
>her eyes fluid and dark and happy
>against the pealing bells of Sheldon Hall.[4]

The Oswego Fugues

This life, this life of eye and weed
and sweat and seed and onion soil—
I see it on green curtains and embossed doors.

I crouch in that yard,
now perfectly overgrown,
and my daughter knows:

> *Daddy, are you crying for them?*
> *Were you a little boy here?*
> *Do you see them, see them still?*

These words will gather

                their fluid arms, their fluid arms,
                flickering in blue devotional candles.
                I never see one remaining still:
                I see Aunt Mary carrying an onion crate,
                my mother ironing clothes all afternoon,
                and my father harvesting lettuce
                by truck lights at night
                to get it to market.
                I see him stand, look up, the face olive, alive.
                I hear him laughing in the fields.
                He and my Grandpa Joe know they
                are getting a fair price. But I see arm on
                arm against the fugue that angels sing.

I see arms:
They rise and fall
and are at last still
in the cool American night,

in the cool American night.
                                      But it makes no sense
                                      then. He owns nothing
                                      but the detonation
                                      in his throat: Listen.

Stephen Murabito
III

I see it now.
Do you see how
I break free from your arms,

the world returned
to pulse and sound?
The families that stand

astonished by it all—
why can I see their hands
at their sides to this day?

And I run to the loft
and look in at the choir:
Cousins Charlie and Mary,

oh, Mrs. Bellardini,
oh, Marie Donabella—
their arms still at their sides.

And I can never tell you
how much I know just then
at the crack of that door,

the voices echoing,
what pulsing comes to me
until you, my breathless mother,

run up the stairs to catch me,
and take me back outside.
The salty light of First Street,

Oswego snow—I live in its
falling, all the way home
to West Eighth and Oneida.

It is 1964. His grandma
has just died, and he
has a "seizure" at her
funeral mass. The small

town doctor says it is
epilepsy. The phenobarbital
says so, too.

They are all in black,
an explosion of stunned
faces, a stillness,
still—a breath of air
passing not to return.[5]

The old woman holds up
her hands, keeps them
all away from him.

This much is given
to him then. There
is no holding it back.

He sees it. He sees it
again. The fleshless
light, the blinding
gravity of death
transposed.

The Oswego Fugues

IV

These words embrace

                the human fire of all their faces,
                faces on bodies and not on walls,
                faces, soft or hard-edged and severe,
                faces, in Italy or Poland, yet in Oswego,
                faces now in the blood surfacing in the blush
                as the light in a huge doorway
                catches our children just so
                or blinds us for that split second
                when photographs are passed, and we spend
                lifetimes in the mind's rush of a second,
                seeing streets, farms, schools,
                or the old man's ruddy and frozen face
                breaking back through that same doorway,
                those small icicles alive in his moustache
                as he holds up his string of lake perch.

These words return

                to my father's uncollectable stories,
                stories present as the bread on your plate.
                He can look at a picture,
                tap it twice like familiar magic,
                nod his head, point to you,
                and take you to Uncle John's farm,
                or deliver Charlie Crisafulli,
                the sharpest dresser in Oswego,
                back before he dies in the war.
                My father, who starts stories
                as if he's never ended them;
                my father, who understands
                the blood of narration;
                my father, whose love is
                the eternal moments between
                the dimensions of rising action;
                my father, who holds histories
                in his hands like doors
                or streets or the three pears
                he will give you when you leave.

                              He sees each story,
                              each pear, each gift.
                              Oh, he hears *the*
                              greater telling!

Stephen Murabito

These words must be

> what I've made,
> what I've become,
> what we've made
> of what we've become:
> Ritual, the human white heat
> of sameness and connection
> to events beyond us
> as we turn in, turn back, turn out,
> turn into our own
> howls and prayers and silences,
> fragments of fact,
> act, song, and breath.

Oh, that split second. We can never hold it.

> It transcends age and face
> and the body in its last fall;
> knowledge, a certain grace,
> given at last to them all.

V

I see Uncle Stosh in his garden.
He weeds and hoes, sending incense
into birdsong, stopping once
to dab the sweat from his eyes.

I stare up at his face,
flames of sweat in a chandelier,
drops of water in a sea of soil.
I see him leaving Warsaw

and feel the bullet hit,
fear palpitating through
his caked and swollen throat.
I hide in the tomatoes

when I visit his garden,
hide until his thick hand
plucks me from the blossoms
of those fruits yet to come.

Oh, he laughs as if he understands.

The Oswego Fugues

But now, I take my turn
to stand in the long line.
I kneel, swearing not to look.

But in the silken casket,
his face is closing downward
as if he is in deepest thought.

Oh, after smoke has risen above
the brass cross of death
strained up by the altar boy,

and after floods of roses,
thinning hands that take them there,
or the way that breathing stops

when your name is called at last,
and you come to say good-bye;
yes, after that last turning

when you are just your steps,
you join beyond your heartbeat
that line that moves to the light.

And now, we recall him
with beer and bread and smoke,

the stories of something spoken,

and the olives breaking on our teeth,

and the sharpest cheese in memory.

He is dead now, Joey.
You must look at what
you've seen for ages.

Inspecting the yellow
blossoms, their promise,
or the frightened kid
knee-deep in the aroma.

Stephen Murabito

VI

> *Have you ever*[6] stood by
> the deep water, the black
> lake, cold, still, and
> lost the fear to dive in,
> as if your children,
> everyone, were between
> the sun, the fish, just
> where the eye stops
> seeing and we begin
> knowing? Have you ever
> stood in the field,
> green, swaying,
> everywhere, and entered the
> fugue, the universal
> music against chaos?[7]
> Have you ever walked to
> that shoreline and felt
> the cold water go warm
> and light at your feet,
> everyone calling you
> home?

Oh, you souls,
what I am allowed to see,
you smiles on dark faces,
you worlds on sweet lips,
you songs in cold beer,
you breaking back again and again—
those behind me, those before me.

Through your hands,
my mind is set ablaze.

He sees through flesh
to the light that is
all there is.

Through your voices
the fugues burn through my ears.

And your voices
hold me forever.

Love, this, this, the
greatest of the three.[8]

And your faces
hold me forever.

The Oswego Fugues

Hold me forever.   This is his tribal
                                              narrative. *Don't let him
go* . . .[9]

             *Shh . . . ita come back to you now.
             And now, you tella everybody.*

Oh, the heaven
of everyone,
the paradise
of this place.

And to think that words
can give birth to a soul.   Look, he's scaling
                                              the rockface. He's
                                              coming out to gaze up
                                              at the stars.[10]

Stephen Murabito

Postlude: Crisis and Confluence

Vince Gotera

Like before, the left and right columns are spoken by the left and right hemispheres of my brain, respectively. The center column features what Stephen Murabito has said about the essential elements of The Oswego Fugues.

The Oswego Fugues is a cogent attempt by one of the strongest of younger contemporary American poets to pursue nothing less than—		
		Hold it, hold it—my brother, my self! Are you trying to peddle that malarkey again?
Well, I thought perhaps the gentle readers "out there" might be ready, now that they have presumably read *The Oswego Fugues,* for our modest but learned interpretation, our *imprimatur—*		
		Let's go slow, all right? How about a comment or two on Steve's craft and technique . . . As Steve pointed out earlier, Joey often speaks in iambs in column one. Look at the start of the poem: "i SEE / my UNcle STOSH" or later, "the WALL, im-MAC-u-LATE."

The Oswego Fugues

Listen closely, folks; this pattern sets us up to notice the first time a crucial repeated phrase is uttered just a few lines later: "Oh, rockface / referentiality" (oh, sorry . . . "oh ROCK-face REF-erEN-ti-AL-it-Y" . . . iambic pentameter spread-eagled across a line break). If we listen carefully to Steve's iambic signposts, knowing we often think of pentameter in particular as signaling seriousness, then our interest is, ideally, piqued by the metric pattern of the phrase "rockface referentiality." But I stray too far ahead. Steve will say more on this in a moment . . .

On a wider note, pertaining to historical influence, *The Oswego Fugues* owes much of its power to William Carlos Williams's collage/montage of a book, *Paterson;* both works are elegies made through impressionist pastiche—impressions, both lyrical and journalistic, on a particular "real" place. Both the good doctor and Professor Murabito use documents, whether actual or fictional: e.g., the text of a letter from a young Allen Ginsberg to Dr. Williams and, in *The Oswego Fugues,* a letter from Joey to one of his college professors, John O'Brien—an actual former teacher of Professor Murabito's at SUNY Oswego.

Throughout the *Fugues,* like that unknown Stonedhenge guitar wizard

Stephen Murabito

whose melodies blaze in my brain like braided flames, Steve's phrasing is like a jazzman's: "Go, you damned and blessed assembly of voices, / You solitary blue note of West Eighth memory. / Go, you sonata of river gull incantation" (from the preface poem, "The Poet, to His Book"). Note the musical hissing of "s" sounds, the more spaced-out repetitions of "bl" and "v," the undercurrent of thrumming "m" and "n."

Another of Professor Murabito's poetic forebears is Wallace Stevens. Note how these lines from "Fugue #2" echo the ending lines of "The Idea of Order at Key West" (an epigraph in the book): "These are our knotted fires, / our twisted, orange shoreline lights, / our philosophies rolled and rolled / long past reason to a paper-thin glow, / then grey ashes dancing, / rising like fireflies, / our questions beyond midnight." It's not only the echo of Stevens's image of the town's "glassy lights"; we have here as well a feeling akin to Stevens's "fiery" passion to pierce through, to find order in a universe that always eludes our grasp.

What I see glimmering in those "knotted fires" and "grey ashes" is this: Steve can craft a mean image. Dig this from "Fugue #4": "a sacred thing, an opus stretched / over the yellow kitchen table: / a thin sheet of strudel dough / draping down like a

The Oswego Fugues

curtain." Or, note the stark haiku-like implosion of this imagistic simile in "Fugue #5": "A garage / door shuts / like a tomb." Talk about vision! Remember that imaginary shrink I pointed to earlier? Voices and visions!

Let's take your having spoken the word "vision" twice here, so serendipitously, as a segue into what Professor Murabito has to say about the central enigma in the book: the vision which Joey feels compelled to unearth, unpack, understand.

Joey's vision: The Oswego Fugues *evokes Dante's* Divine Comedy *in its first main epigraph and Robert Pirsig's* Zen and the Art of Motorcycle Maintenance *in its second main epigraph. Both quotes speak to journeys, struggles, the working toward a deep vision.* The Oswego Fugues *is, ultimately, a poem about the exfoliation of a vision, the vision that "breaks back" to Joey and to the reader a piece at time. As Mrs. Zicci says to the young Joey when he has his vision:*

> It'sa ok. Ita leave you now.
> Ita come back somma day.
> Shh . . . somma day, you know,
> And you tella everybody.

This vision is that we walk with the dead; they are among us as we are all passing in confluences of mind and light. Essentially, he sees the dead, and he sees the dead within the living. The entire thrust of the poem is the piece-by-piece unfolding of this vision—can Joey face it and say it? And, moreover, can he find the words to express the inexpressible?

This dilemma is precisely at the center of Toni Morrison's novel *Beloved*. "See[ing] the dead within the living" whether literally or in some ghostly way. In that novel, Morrison also uses "piece-by-piece unfolding," endlessly circling around the truth.

Whether "truth" in some philosophical fashion (or even in lexical denotation) can be grasped or not—that is one of the most thorny problems of postructural literary theory. Can we ever connect the signifier and the signified? Is there a signified behind the signifier? Or does the slippage between them disclose so vast an abyss we can never connect?

The main refrain of the poem is exactly this issue—"rockface referentiality"—one of the most burning and unsolved modernist questions. Can a language be found to express our experience? This idea is set into motion from the very first epigraph to "Fugue #1," from Wallace Stevens's "The Idea of Order at Key West." Among other things, then, the book wrestles with the idea of referentiality, and in "Fugue #6," Joey is able to join all of the voices while he has captured the essences of those around him as he sees Oswego and these people as portals to Paradise. He stops saying "these words refer to . . ." and now says "these words are . . ." showing us the lives and deaths and meanings of these souls.

One of the most striking memories of my childhood is sparked by words Steve says here: "Paradise," "lives and deaths," "souls." I remember sneaking into my grandfather's study and getting down a heavy book—I can still smell its unique odor, an amalgam of dust and ancient paper, melding in my child's mind with sulfur and smoke. Dante's *Divine Comedy,* with those phenomenal engravings by Gustave Doré. I was very worried about (and by) those sinners in the inferno who eternally tear their own chests open, their frail hearts beating in brimstone air.

Dante is crucial to *The Oswego Fugues* for many reasons. Just as Joey Bernardo is on a search to make sense of his life, Dante Alighieri finds himself in a dark wood, in a midlife crisis (as we say now), trying to make sense of not only his own life but of the afterlife he is shown. Both characters are on a quest; as Joseph Campbell's idea of the "monomyth"

Stephen Murabito

codifies, both of these quest heroes are on a journey outward, wherein they must overcome certain obstacles in order to earn and bring back a "boon"—i.e., a gift to enlighten the lives of others. Dante's quest ends in the stars, and so does Joey's: The chorus at the end of the book says, "Look, he's scaling / the rockface. He's / coming out to gaze up / at the stars." Joey finds a usable *referential* language, "words [that] embrace / the human fire of all their faces / . . . lifetimes in the mind's rush of a second." He finds linguistic communion, allowing him to merge with/in the totality of the quick and the dead, like Dante marveling at the luminous rose-shape the angels make in the firmament, like Eliot's "crowned knot of fire" (in "Little Gidding"), where "the fire and the rose are one." Joey's personal *stretto maestrale* is "Oh, the heaven / of everyone, / the paradise / of this place." And this place is Oswego. Belonging. Longing. Being. Home.

So The Oswego Fugues *is an ecstatic poem that is not religious in any way. It is the capturing of a vision and the birth of a soul. It ends as it begins, evoking Dante as the speaker joins all of the other voices that comprise him, his home, and indeed life.*

The Oswego Fugues

In what I hope you will agree is a "metapoem," Steve's gloss on the *Fugues* in the middle column, he proposes one more thing:

The fugues overall present this vision, this quest, as each fugue also deals with other limited, focused themes:

- *"Fugue #1" — Family*
- *"Fugue #2" — Place*
- *"Fugue #3" — Making and The Other*
- *"Fugue #4" — Education and Learning*
- *"Fugue #5" — Love and Death*
- *"Fugue #6" — Referentiality and Soul*

As we all learned in our first English-major classes (those of us who had the fortune—or misfortune—to be English majors), you're on pretty shaky ground trying to psych out a writer's intention (the dreaded "intentional fallacy"), even when the writer tells you straight out, as Steve has done. After all, there may be all sorts of factors invisible to the writer, lodged in the subconscious. Given that caveat, I'll leave it up to you, good readers, if you want to take Steve's word on these other "limited themes." Fallacies notwithstanding, however, the movement Steve suggests here is a spiraling one from innocence to wisdom: from the bosom of the "family," through

Stephen Murabito

Can I say it now?

The Oswego Fugues is a cogent attempt by one of the strongest of younger contemporary American poets to pursue nothing less than a paradigm shift beyond postmodernity, beyond the poststructural, taking into account the metaphysical and philosophical paradigms which came before, dramatizing the individual and collective human quest for vision, voice, verity.

explorations of "place" (our own Oswegos), to our first experiences with "making" (recall that the root meaning of "poet" is "maker"), to our initial conflicts and embraces with "others." We study and learn, we fall in love and prepare to die, and ultimately we must all wrestle with who we were, are, and will be, in order to (as *The Oswego Fugues* says at the end) "give birth to a soul."

Go ahead.

Fugue it, baby. *Stretto maestrale:* straight, master the role / stride the mistral / strut the mystery—the real. Amen. Oh man. Om. Home.

The Oswego Fugues

Biographical Note:

Poet, critic, teacher, and editor, Vince Gotera's books include a recent chapbook of poems occasioned by the US war in Iraq, *Ghost Wars* (Final Thursday Press), and a literary critical study, *Radical Visions: Poems by Vietnam Veterans* (University of Georgia Press). He teaches creative writing and literature at the University of Northern Iowa, where he also serves as Editor at the *North American Review* (the oldest American literary magazine, established in 1815).

Stephen Murabito

The Oswego Fugues

Notes

Fugue One: "Places Where the Train Stopped"

1. My source is *Modern American Poetry,* edited by Louis Untermeyer, Harcourt, Brace, and World, 1958, pp. 249-50. Wallace Stevens's poem serves as a major motif throughout the entire *Oswego Fugues.* Among other vital things, "The Idea of Order at Key West" asks what art is for and why the artist attempts to capture the experience of a vision. Stevens's poem also asks the modernist question of whether language can capture anything in the first place. As his poem says, the artist has a "rage for order" as well as a "rage to order," and words or pieces of any art can become "fragrant portals" because of the potential of words or any art to show us other worlds; however, art or that other world can remain so "dimly-starred" because of the inevitable limits of art to capture completely. Art obviously becomes successful and potentially great when it meets or even transcends these various limits, this "rockface/referentiality" as my speaker calls it.

   This is really the dilemma of my main speaker, the young man occupying the far left column. When he was a child, he had a tremendous vision, and the poem is really about how he comes to terms with and embraces that vision. In Stevens's poem, the question is how do we wring order from chaos; in my poem, the question is how does a speaker bring confluence and beautiful alignment to the voices, faces, and souls comprising that vision?

   Also, in a note about the structure of the fugues themselves, I am working with three columns: The far left is the main speaker; the middle is either the speaker or the voices of characters; and the far right is meant to operate as yet a third voice, something more detatched, like a Greek chorus, an entity that can be both serious and humorous.

2. The "ring size" of a cigar is its width, its thickness. Number fifty-two is a big one, almost one inch thick. Hoyo De Monterey is a fine Honduran cigar.

3. Quite literally, this is half of the famous imagistic poem by Ezra Pound, "In A Station of the Metro." My source is the good old *Norton Anthology of Modern Poetry*, edited by Richard Ellmann and Robert O'Clair, W. W. Norton, 1973, p. 338.

The Oswego Fugues

4. This is from John Donne's great "A Valediction: Forbidding Mourning," in *John Donne: The Complete Poems*, edited by A. J. Smith, 1971, Penguin, p. 84.

5. From William Wordsworth's "Lines Composed a Few Miles Above Tintern Abbey," in the *Norton Anthology of Poetry*, Fourth Edition, edited by Margaret Ferguson, Mary Jo Salter, and Jon Stallworthy, 1996, p. 701.

⌘ ⌘ ⌘

Fugue Two: "The Scene That Forgot the Man"

1. This comes from Robert Pinsky's book-length poem, *An Explanation of America*, published by Princeton University Press, 1979, p. 19.

2. John O'Brien, a friend and ex-teacher of mine at SUNY Oswego.

3. These indented and italicized lines are all from the earlier-noted Robert Pinsky epigraph.

4. This is the glove from the cover of John Logan's *Only the Dreamer Can Change the Dream: Selected Poems*, Ecco Press, 1981.

5. These lines are from "Two Preludes for La Push," in John Logan's *Dreamer . . .* , p. 112.

⌘ ⌘ ⌘

Fugue Three: "The Echoes We Come to Embrace"

1. As I traveled around in Oswego, NY, in June of 1992, I heard this when I came to a stop at a corner on the Westside.

2. This comes from a letter originally printed in *Briefe aus derr Jahren, 1907-1914* (Leipzig: Insel-Verlag, 1933). My source is *Duino Elegies*, translated by Stephen Garmey and Jay Wilson, Harper and Row, 1972, p. 8.

3. These lines are from Ezra Pound's "Piere Vidal Old," which appears in *Personae: Collected Shorter Poems*, New Directions, 1971, p. 31.

Stephen Murabito

4. This is the long-respected source on formal poetry (E. P. Dutton, 1968) by Lewis Putnam Turco, a professor of mine at Oswego State University from 1979 to 1981.

5. This line comes from Emily Dickinson's short quatrain "'Faith' is a fine invention." My source is *The Complete Poems of Emily Dickinson*, edited by Thomas H. Johnson, Little, Brown, and Company, 1960, pp. 87-88.

6. Again, this is from Wallace Stevens's "The Idea of Order at Key West." All subsequent italicized lines also come from "Idea . . ."

7. I get this idea of "selective" or even "inventive" memory from a 1992 interview with Terry Prior, Director, Oswego County Historical Society. I thank Terry for bringing me on a tour of the Richardson-Bates House on East Third Street.

8. This quote about Bach comes from the notes on the following album: Winograd String Orchestra, J.S. Bach's *The Art of the Fugue*. Heliodor H/HS 25019-2; MGM 2-3E. Notes by Edward Cole.

9. This is quoted in Jan Chiapusso's *Bach's World*. Indiana University Press, 1968, p. 152.

10. Olson says this in "Projective Verse," which appears in *The Poetics of the New American Poetry*, edited by Donald Allen and Warren Tallman, Grove Press, 1973, p. 149.

11. This again references Rainer Maria Rilke's *Duino Elegies* as above cited in Note Number Two.

12. *stretto maestrale* is a critical term often used in the discussion and analysis of musical fugues. It is the moment when the different voices are following one another to a conclusion; it is the phenomenon of the voices working toward their final climax, their ultimate integration. My source is *The Norton/Grove Concise Encyclopaedia of Music*, edited by Stanley Sadie, W. W. Norton, 1994, p. 785.

⌘ ⌘ ⌘

Fugue Four: "The Wonderful Chaos"

1. Michael True's "Syllabus" comes from *College Composition and Communication*, Volume 29, 1978, p. 248.

The Oswego Fugues

2. This is Edward Austin Sheldon, American educator and founder of the Oswego Normal School, which later became the State University of New York, College at Oswego.

3. I originally attended SUNY Oswego in 1974. I promptly failed out of school due to drinking and not studying. Later, the same things overwhelmingly contributed to my academic success.

4. This line and all italicized lines that follow come from the True poem.

5. This definition is from *Webster's New World Dictionary*, Third College Edition, p. 1384.

6. These lines are Virgil's admonition to Dante. They are previously identified as the epigraph of the *Oswego Fugues*. The best existing translation of Canto XXIV, 43-60, is to be found in *The Inferno*, translated by John Ciardi, reprinted as a Signet Classic, 2001, p. 207.

7. This quote from Henry James is in David Madden's anthology *The World of Fiction*. Holt, Rinehart, Winston, 1990, p. 1131.

8. See *The English Poems of George Herbert*, Dent, 1974, p. 186.

9. *Cinoti* is one of the most ancient terms for "poet." The word (from the Sanskrit) meant he arranges or he piles up. A modern interpretation might be he who makes lists or catalogues. Professor Cinoti, then, is obviously a fictional character whose name signifies the archetypal nature of her essence.

10. Dr. David Harbert was a philosophy professor of mine at SUNY Oswego. He died in February of 1993. The test without a question was a reality.

11. This etymology of the name Oswego comes from Lewis H. Morgan's *League of the Iroquois*, reprinted, Corinth, 1962, p. 395. Morgan gives the following Iroquois dialect renderings for Oswego: Seneca: Swa-geh´; Cayuga: Swa-geh´; Onondaga: Swa-geh´; Tuscarora: O-swa´-geh; Oneida: O-swage´-ga; Mohawk: O-swa´-go. Morgan's "signification" of the word is "flowing out." In this regard, it is like the above-mentioned definition of text: "thing from act / unending process."

12. These lines are from Lewis Putnam Turco's "The College," which appears in *The Shifting Web: New and Selected Poems*, University of Arkansas Press, 1989, p. 91.

Stephen Murabito

⌘ ⌘ ⌘

Fugue Five: "Young Lovers Stand There Against Saint Stephen's"

1. These are the closing lines of Rainer Maria Rilke's Third Duino Elegy (source: the above-mentioned text of Garmey and Wilson). To say what Rilke means is difficult, and to hear his own explanations might not be much help, either. What I mean is the human desire not to let a loved one go, an urge which seeks to keep love alive in the smallest, most familiar ways. These are the ways we know places, others, and ourselves. Rilke's words are among the most beautiful ever written because they are so simple yet so spiritually complex. He is speaking of love, simplicity, of the everyday, the ultimately known and felt, yet the spiritual—the things, all told, which make us realize our humanity: Lovers do not want to let one another go; parents do not want to let their children go; the returned never want to let places go; and the speaker does not want to let the old woman go.

2. These are streets of the Polish Hill section of Oswego, NY.

3. See above, Fugue Number Three, Note Twelve.

4. These lines are from "Exequy," which appears in *The Poems of Henry King*, edited by Margaret Crum, Oxford University Press, 1965, pp. 68-72.

5. These lines come from Part One of Virginia Woolf's *To the Lighthouse*. My edition is Harcourt Brace, and World, 1927, p. 33.

⌘ ⌘ ⌘

Fugue Six: "The Greater Telling"

1. The Li-Young Lee poem comes from *The City in Which I Love You*, BOA Editions, 1990, pp. 13-29. The collection was the Lamont Poetry Selection for 1990. Later in this fugue, another reference to these lines is marked in italics.

2. "What Song, Then?" comes from Kathleen Norris's *Little Girls in Church*, University of Pittsburgh Press, 1999, p. 55.

3. The above-mentioned Rainer Maria Rilke is referenced here again.

The Oswego Fugues

4. Sheldon Hall, earlier mentioned, is the beautiful main building on the SUNY Oswego campus. It is no longer an academic building; it now is a convention center.

5. A paraphrase of Psalm 78:39: "He remembered that they were but mortal, a breath of air which passes by and does not return." *The Revised English Bible*, Oxford and Cambridge University Presses, 1989, p. 508.

6. *Have you ever* comes from the Robert Creeley Poem "Dreams," which is in *Windows*, New Directions, 1990, pp. 63-64. Here's the third and closing section:

> Have you ever
> had a vision as if
>
> you were walking
> forward to some
>
> edge of water through
> the trees, some country
>
> sunlit lane, some
> place was just ahead
>
> and opening as your body
> elsewhere came
>
> and you had
> been in two places?

7. The idea that there is a universal music, and that it is present as a constant natural force against chaos and entropy, is put forth by Lewis Thomas in "The Music of This Sphere," which appears in *The Lives of a Cell*, Viking/Penguin, 1974, pp. 20-25. The penultimate paragraph is distinctive:

> If, as I believe, the urge to make a kind of music is as much a characteristic of biology as our other fundamental functions, there ought to be an explanation for it. Having none at hand, I am free to make one up. The rhythmic sounds might be a recapitulation of something else—an earliest memory, a score for the transformation of inanimate, random

matter in chaos into the improbable, ordered dance of living forms. Morowitz has presented the case, in thermodynamic terms, for the hypothesis that a steady flow of energy from the inexhaustible source of the sun to the unfillable sink of outer space, by way of the earth, is mathematically destined to cause the organization of matter into an increasingly ordered state. The resulting balancing act involves a ceaseless clustering of bonded atoms into molecules of higher and higher complexity, and the emergence of cycles for the storage and release of energy. In a nonequilibrium steady state, which is postulated, the solar energy would not just flow to earth and radiate away; it is thermodynamically inevitable that it must rearrange matter into symmetry, away from probability, against entropy, lifting it, so to speak, into a constant changing condition of rearrangement and molecular ornamentation. In such a system, the outcome is a chancy kind of order, always on the verge of descending into chaos, held taut against probability by the unremitting, constant surge of energy from the sun.

8. In 1 Cor. 13:13, Saint Paul says, "There are three things that last forever: faith, hope, and love; and the greatest of the three is love." My source is the above-mentioned *Revised English Bible*, p. 156.

9. Again, Rilke.

10. These are the final lines of Dante's *Inferno*, after he emerges from his journey with Virgil. Again, I am thinking of John Ciardi's translation of Canto XXXIV in the Signet Classic, p. 287.

⌘ ⌘ ⌘

The Oswego Fugues

Stephen Murabito

Photo by Estella Marie Murabito

A native of Oswego, New York, Stephen Murabito is an associate professor of English at the University of Pittsburgh at Greensburg. He was a National Endowment for the Arts fellow in poetry in 1992. His poems and stories have appeared widely in such periodicals as *Beloit Poetry Journal, Mississippi Review, 5AM,* and *Poet Lore; North American Review, Brooklyn Review, Caketrain,* and *Antietam Review*. He is the author of the poetry chapbook *A Little Dinner Music* (Parallel Press, 2004), and he is the author/editor of the composition reader *Connections, Contexts, and Possibilities* (Prentice Hall, 2001). He lives in Saltsburg, Pennsylvania, with his wife, April, and their four children—Angelina, Estella, Antonia, and Sebastian.

The Oswego Fugues

Stephen Murabito

www.ingramcontent.com/pod-product-compliance
Lightning Source LLC
Chambersburg PA
CBHW081840170426
43199CB00017B/2790